M

in a
Peacock Parade:

A Funny Thing Happened
On the Way to Heaven

Dan R. Crawford

HANNIBAL BOOKS
www.hannibalbooks.com

"The Swan" joins "The Mud Hen" in the Comedy of Life's Parade!! And you need to jump into the line-up with us! So here's what you do: Grab a cup of dark-roast coffee—doctor it up a tad—and find your favorite chair and consume some GREAT comedic commentaries on life provided by Dr. Mud Hen himself—Dr. Reverend "not so holy" Professor Dan Crawford. Dan gives us "laughter" with plenty of "life" on it! Matter of fact, it might be just the Medicine you need for what ails ya! So put the channel changer up . . . you won't need it—MUD HEN IN A PEACOCK PARADE will replace the "one eyed monster"!

Dr. Dennis "The Swan" Swanberg
America's Minister of Encouragement
www.dennisswanberg.com

Laughter is good medicine (Prov. 17:22). Dan Crawford provides us with some of the best of that kind of medicine with true humorous stories from his position with a wonderful seminary in which academic excellence and, yes, a rollicking sense of humor are required.

Al Fasol
retired professor of preaching
Southwestern Baptist Seminary
Author, *Humor with a Halo*

My first idea as I think of these funny events is: "Truth is stranger than fiction." Those who know Dan Crawford know that he's not actively looking for funny stories. They just happen, and he's there to report them. It's been my privilege to be with him when some of the funny stories "happened." Readers will enjoy this book because most will recall having been there, done that.

Gerre Joiner
retired minister of music
Decatur, TX

3

Published by
Hannibal Books
PO Box 461592
Garland, Texas 75046-1592
Copyright Dan R. Crawford 2009
All Rights Reserved
Printed in the United States of America

Cover design by Dennis Davidson
Except where otherwise indicated, all Scripture taken from the Holy Bible,
New King James Version, copyright 1979 and 1980
by Thomas Nelson Publishers
ISBN 978-1-934749-47-0
Library of Congress Control Number: 2009924434

TO ORDER ADDITIONAL COPIES, SEE PAGE 143

Dedicated to
those who have helped me laugh
when crying would have been easier

Table of Contents

An Explanation of the Book Title
Mud Hen in a Peacock Parade

While enduring a boring graduation speech, the inspiration for this book popped into my head. A few days earlier I had received a call from the university president's office. The call informed me that this particular year was a Baptist year to pray at graduation. Since I was the Baptist campus minister, I accepted the invitation. Graduation at the University of Texas at Austin is held outside on the mall in front of the Main Building, better known as the University Tower. Program personalities sit on the steps of the tower with the audience facing the main entrance to the building. Inscribed in stone over the door—and clearly visible to the graduation audience— are the words of Jesus recorded in John 8:32, *"You shall know the truth, and the truth shall make you free."* I had decided to include that in my invocation. As the procession began I was introduced to the speaker, the president of another very highly regarded academic institution. My place in the processional was between the speaker and the president of the University of Texas. They each had several academic degrees, so their robes were adorned with many colors. We were followed by the university's faculty members adorned in their robes of many colors. I had not yet completed my doctor's degree, so I marched in a black robe, with black hat. Someone commented that I looked like a *mud hen in a peacock parade.*

As the graduation ceremony continued, I tried desperately to stay awake, since I was seated on the platform in front of hundreds of graduates and their families. Graduation speeches are notoriously boring. Garry Trudeau, author of the *Doonesbury* comic strip, once said, "Graduation speeches were invented largely in the belief that college students should never be released into the world until they have been properly sedated."

In the midst of one of the most boring graduation addresses I had ever heard (and I have heard dozens of them), I began to think of other interesting experiences in my life. Somehow every experience that sprang to my mind reminded me of that *mud hen surrounded by peacocks.* I have often been in over my head but thankfully never over my heart. And God has granted me a wonderful sense of humor that allows me to see the fun side of almost everything. So while some have found their life paths full of negatives, I have envisioned mine as a series of funny things happening on my way to heaven.

But let's get back to the commencement service. In my invocation I had quoted the verse inscribed over the door and thanked God for the pursuit of truth in which the university was engaged and also the Truth that sets us free. In the midst of the graduation speech the speaker made an eye-opening statement, "Now I must correct the Rev. Mr. Crawford from his prayer earlier. Truth is relative. It is not embodied in any person." Most were asleep when he made this bold statement, but he sure got my attention. I stopped worrying when I remembered that I was also responsible for the benediction.

An old Southern expression says "Church ain't over until the fat lady sings." As the Texas A&M University basketball team tied the Texas Tech Red Raiders at the buzzer in the final game of the 1976 Southwest Conference Tournament, announcer Ralph Carpenter said, "The opera ain't over   'till the fat lady sings." Various sports announcers picked up the phrase saying, "The game ain't over 'till the fat lady sings."[1] Well, graduation wasn't over 'till the Mud Hen prayed—the second time! Go Mud Hens!

[1] From *Wikipedia: The Free Encyclopedia.*
http://en.wikipedia.org/wiki/Fat lady

Preface

A preface is a pre-face. That image in itself could produce laughter. What is pre-face? What comes prior to a face; is preliminary to a face; precedes a face? Perhaps pre-face is a blank look, a solemn expression, a neutral emotion. Whatever it is, it is a pre-laughing face. So, before we laugh, let's be serious for a brief time.

In the Bible you arrive at the 17th chapter of Genesis to read, *"Then Abraham fell on his face and laughed"* (Gen. 17:17). In the first reference to laughter in human history, Abraham was laughing at what he thought was a joke, that a 100-year-old-man and a 90-year-old-woman could produce a child. When Sarah heard the announcement, she joined her husband and, *"laughed within herself"* (Gen. 18:12). Then, displaying a wonderful sense of humor, she named the child Isaac, meaning "laughter", and proclaimed, *"God has made me laugh, and all who hear will laugh with me"* (Gen. 21:3, 6). Shared laughter is always better than solo laughter. Although no Scripture reference to it exists, I suspect God had the last laugh on this subject.

The word of the Lord concerning Sennacherib included this statement: *The daughter of Zion has despised you, laughed you to scorn* (2 Kings 19:21).

In the midst of Job's suffering his friend, Bildad, offered words of encouragement. He said of God, *"He will yet fill your mouth with laughing, and your lips with rejoicing"* (Job 8:21). Interestingly enough, in this book of the Bible with so much suffering, trial, and grief, laughter is mentioned six times.

Balancing the wrath, judgment, vengeance, and anger of God, the psalmist proclaims, *He who sits in the heavens shall laugh* (Ps. 2:4). This is the first of seven references to laughter in this Hebrew hymnbook. It would not be the last time music would provide joy and laughter.

In the wisdom literature of the Old Testament laughter is mentioned three times in Proverbs. Among his four references to laughter the writer of Ecclesiastes offers a sample list of *"every purpose under heaven"*—listing *"a time to laugh"* as one of the purposes (Eccl. 3:1, 4).

Twice in the serious writing of the Hebrew prophets, laughter is mentioned—once in Isaiah and once in Ezekiel.

Before Jesus raised the daughter of Jairus from the dead, Matthew, Mark, and Luke all record that the people laughed at the idea that she was only sleeping.

In Luke's version of the Sermon on the Mount he remembered Jesus saying, *"Blessed are you who weep now, for you shall laugh."* Then a few verses later he quotes Jesus as saying, *"Woe to you who laugh now, for you shall mourn and weep"* (Luke 6:21, 25). Indeed, we have a proper and correct time to laugh.

The final reference to laughter in the Bible is in the midst of the New Testament epistles in the letter of James.

I believe Jesus enjoyed life. I have no problem imagining Him laughing with His disciples—or even at them. He was constantly criticizing the religious leaders for their serious legalism and their self-righteous lifestyle. Yet His humor was not designed to hurt as is some of today's humor. I agree with an earlier British writer who concluded, "It is very important to understand that the evident purpose of Christ's humor is to clarify and increase understanding, rather than hurt."[1]

To fail to recognize, enjoy, and even emulate the humor of our Lord is to miss much of the joy of life. In his classic book, *The Humor of Christ*, Elton Trueblood, wrote:

"The widespread failure to recognize and to appreciate the

humor of Christ is one of the most amazing aspects of the era named for Him. Anyone who reads the Synoptic Gospels with a relative freedom from presuppositions might be expected to see that Christ laughed, and that He expected others to laugh, but our capacity to miss this aspect of His life is phenomenal. We are so sure that he was always deadly serious that we often twist His words in order to try to make them conform to our preconceived mold. A misguided piety has made us fear that acceptance of His obvious wit and humor would somehow be mildly blasphemous or sacrilegious. Religion, we think, is serious business, and serious business in incompatible with banter."2

Likewise, Henri Cormier wrote, "Jesus has a sense of humor. Even today in us and in our midst He wants to show that sense of humor."3

Granted, life is not just one big laugh. Most of life is serious; some is solemn. As the writer of Ecclesiastes expressed, we have a time for weeping as well as a time for laughter.

The purpose of this book is not to diminish the value of seriousness nor to de-emphasize the need for weeping. Rather my purpose is to exalt the blessedness of laughter and joy.

Leslie Weatherhead wrote, "The opposite of joy is not sorrow. It is unbelief."4 We believe, therefore in the value of joy and the potential for proper laughter. Believers have more reason to laugh than anyone does. Indeed, more genuine joy exists at a Christian funeral than at a non-Christian party.

In preparation for this book I read various articles and books on the subject of laughter. Some were helpful. Others made me laugh. I tried to think seriously when I read, "researchers have tried to prove laughter results from detecting incongruities or responding to humorous stimuli." I seriously did not understand what that meant, so I laughed. Then I read, "Studies have found laughing comparable to progressive relaxation and minor analgesics in reducing stress and pain." Wanting to reduce stress and pain I liked what I understood about that statement.

In his book, *Laughter: A Scientific Investigation*, Robert R. Provine, professor of psychology at the University of Maryland, offers the following guidelines for inviting laughter into your life:

"Be social. When you build friendships, you're building laughter. The best way to start yourself laughing is to find someone to laugh with.

"Seek out groups. The old adage, *the more the merrier*, is true. A large crowd laughs more than a small one.

"Follow the sound of laughter. Laughter is contagious, so put yourself in situations where you'll catch it.

"Lower your laughter threshold. We tend to do this automatically in certain situations. If you are with someone who once made you laugh, you expect to repeat the experience. Once you're primed for laughter, even mild humor may seem hysterical.

"Keep funny things around—photographs, joke books, movies you've enjoyed, etc.. . . . or something that connects you to another person even in his/her absence, such as a funny card the person sent to you. Such items can be potent pick-me-ups, so make them readily available for when you need them most.

"Think beyond your own laughter. A sense of humor, a trait admired by everyone, refers not to your yuks and titers, but to your ability to give the gift of laughter. Laughter is a gift that is always returned with interest."[5]

Further demonstrating the value of laughter is a wonderful story originally reported in the *New England Journal of Medicine* in 1976 and more recently retold by my good friend Dan Pryor in his newsletter, *SpeedBumps*.[6] Norman Cousins, former editor of the *Saturday Review*, was stricken in 1964 with *ankylosing spondylitis*, a serious, painful, connective tissue disease. He concluded his traditional treatment of hospitalization and medication was not adequate. Each day his friends brought old reels of *Candid Camera* and Marx Brothers movies, which they watched together in his hospital room. Cousins found that 10 minutes of belly laughs provided him two hours of restful, pain-free sleep. When his "degree of inflammation" was measured after a hearty laughing spell, it measured a significant decrease.

As Grady Nutt, "The Prime Minister of Humor" on the old television program *Hee Haw,* often said, "Laughter is the hand of God on the shoulder of a troubled world."

And Rick Warren, author of *The Purpose Driven Life,* wrote in his *Ministry ToolBox:*

"Humor is an amazing thing. It's a tension dissolver. It's an antidote to anxiety. It's just like a tranquilizer, but without any troublesome side effects. And it's free! You don't even need a prescription. Laughter is life's shock absorber. If you want to have less stress in your life, learn to laugh at your circumstances. Somehow, you must find the fun in frustrating (circumstances) . . . .. If you can laugh at it, you can live with it."[7]

Robert A. Emmons, professor of psychology at the University of California at Davis and a leading scholar of positive psychology, conducted an analysis of hundreds of psychological studies. He concluded, "Our lives do not just seem better when we are happy—they actually become better. Happy people tend to live longer, have more loving marriages, are healthier, live an average of seven to nine years longer than chronically unhappy people, and have more successful careers."[8]

But enough seriousness! Democritus was known as the "Laughing Philosopher of Abde'ra." He was a Greek philosopher who developed one of the first atomist theories of the universe and espoused the doctrine that pleasure along with self-control is the goal of human life. But he began to take things too seriously. He reportedly put out his eyes so that he might think more deeply. Don't do that.

Read and enjoy. Laugh at me. Laugh with me. Laugh around me. Laugh behind my back. Laugh over my head. But, for goodness' sake, laugh! Among other benefits, it will make your journey to heaven more enjoyable and heaven more recognizable.

[1] D.N. Morison, *The Humour of Christ* (London, 1931).

[2] Elton Trueblood, *The Humor of Christ* (New York: Harper & Row, Publishers, 1964), 15.

[3] Henri Cormier, *The Humor of Jesus* (Staten Island, NY: Alba House, 1977), xii.

[4] Leslie Weatherhead, *This is Victory* (Nashville: Abingdon Press, 1941), 171.

[5] Robert R. Provine, *Laughter: A Scientific Investigation* (New York: Viking Penguin, 2000).

[6] "Laughter in a Hurting World," *SpeedBumps,* Dan & Nancy Pryor, Editors, P.O. Box 820904, Dallas, TX, 75382-0904. October 2001.

[7] "Learn to Laugh" by Rick Warren. *Rick Warren's Ministry ToolBox,* Issue #319, July, 11, 2007, 1.

[8] "Science Discovers the Secret to Happiness" by Robert A. Emmons. *Bottom Line Retirement.* Volume 15, Number 8. August 2008, p.1.

Chapter One

Early Laughter

King's Daughters Hospital in Temple, TX, had a tradition of placing one newborn baby each day in a special show-window. While all newborns were visible to the adoring eyes of family and friends, the show-window baby was designated as special. I am told I was left in that special window for one week. Based on my appearance through the years I am fairly certain I was not left in the window because of good looks. It must have been my pleasant disposition! Or then again it may have been the fact that my mother was a registered nurse at the same hospital. Nevertheless I began in the spotlight with people making funny faces at me and laughing. Not many of those people are still around, but none of them would be surprised that I would write a book allowing and encouraging people to laugh at me. So allow me to put myself in the show-window once again. Laugh at your leisure.

Amen—sit down!

Because my father was the pastor, I grew up in and around the church. While other kids my age were experiencing laughter in various places, most of my laughter took place at church. When you start going to church activities at an early age, misunderstanding some things is easy. We seemed to often hear Greek words from the Bible. So whenever we heard a word we did not understand, we assumed it must be a Greek word. I did not understand the word "Amen." All I knew was that every time anyone said "Amen," people sat down. So I grew up thinking "Amen" was a Greek word meaning "sit down."

It runs in the family

When the Crawford family gathered, the occasion always included generous helpings of food and fun. The fun usually began immediately on the arrival of the first family member. The food was usually spread around the kitchen and served all-you-can-eat buffet style. At one family Christmas dinner my grandfather did an exceptional job overloading his plate at the buffet table. He was reminded he didn't have to get all of his food on his first time through the buffet line but could go back to the kitchen for seconds. He replied, "No thanks! I've eaten with this family before. There likely won't be anything left in the kitchen when I get ready for seconds."

Christmas confusion

One December during my childhood the teachers at our church were having us draw pictures of Christmas. They asked us to emphasize in our artwork the importance of the spiritual parts of our celebration. I had no trouble drawing baby Jesus and the manger. However, one kid, who attended church only occasionally, drew his picture complete with a round, chubby character looking around the corner of the manger. When asked who the fat figure was, the kid replied, "Round John Virgin!"

Nice catch!

Men-and-boy fishing trips were always worth a few laughs. Someone usually fell into the lake or river or got pushed in. Older boys always seemed to try to convince the younger boys how good the bait tasted. The men always seemed to do more fishing than the boys did. One wondered for whom these trips were really designed! I'll never forget the year one of the men landed a 55-pound catch. He only needed a few minutes to reel in his catch. Of course, over an hour was necessary to get the hook out of the kid's arm.

I didn't know that!

Even my baptism provided a bit of humor. I obviously was excited about being baptized and could hardly wait to tell everyone I knew. On Monday morning I delighted in explaining to my third-grade teacher all about my Sunday-night baptism. She listened with detached interest. No smile. No congratulations. No emotion. I was puzzled since everyone else had shared in my excitement and been extremely affirming. That night when I asked my parents what was wrong with my teacher, they informed me she was Jewish. I didn't know that!

Football fiasco

On Wednesday evenings at church we always had our mission activities followed by prayer meeting. If we attended the mission activity and had our memory work done, we were allowed to play football during prayer meeting, which seemed a far better use of a boy's time. The football field was next to the auditorium where the prayer meeting was held. Actually it was next to the beautiful and expensive stained-glass windows of the auditorium where the prayer meeting was held. On fourth down, Mark White, who about 30 years later would be elected governor of Texas, punted for our team. The football went off the side of his foot toward the stained-glass windows. For what seemed to be an eternity, a group of mission-minded, football-player wannabees watched in horror—anticipating the first known excommunication of youth from a Baptist church. Somehow, the football glanced off the windows without any harm being done. When asked why he kicked the ball into the windows, Mark explained, "Crawford made a bad snap from center." I remember thinking then, "Mark ought to go into politics when he grows up."

Hospital humor

When I was 15-years old, I was in an automobile accident with four other teen-agers from our church. We were on our way to a church-sponsored hayride and had become lost. We made a left turn and then stopped after we realized we had made a mistake. As we waited for the traffic to clear before we backed onto the highway, a speeding driver under the heavy influence of alcohol left the highway and hit our car with such force that we spun around in the air several times before the car rested. When the car landed, I no longer was in it. I was in a water-filled drainage ditch. Later I was diagnosed with a broken second vertebra of the neck. The recovery time was nine months.

While I experienced many days of disappointment and tears during the recovery, I also had days of joy and laughter. I remember looking at the hospital ceiling fan one day and wondering how many tissues I could throw and make land on the fan's blades. I gave it a try, with my mother picking up all of my mistakes. I'm not sure how many tissues I finally got on the blades, but I do remember a very stern and serious nurse coming into the room to ask if I needed anything. "Sure do!" I said. "It's really warm in here. Could you please turn on the ceiling fan?" I'll never forget the look on her face when it began to snow tissues all over that room. When you have a choice between laughter and crying, laughter usually is the better selection!

Speaking of hayrides

In the preceding story, I mentioned a hayride. I realize that younger readers may not understand this term, especially if they have been reared in an urban setting. Let me begin by explaining a theory adults during my youth widely held about rearing teen-agers. That theory held that if our church leaders and parents could keep us busy at church, we would not have time to sin. One of the many activities invented by adults in their attempt to keep us pure was the hayride. For the hayride a wagon or flatbed truck was secured. Hay was purchased or donated from someone's country relative. A cool night with a full moon was selected. And young people with far too few chaperones went riding on the hay in the moonlight. Well, it kept us involved in church activities. Unfortunately, most people my age who were active churchgoers in their teens learned to sin on hayrides

Summer church camp

Another activity designed to keep us busy was the summer church camp. For me, it was an annual July week on the Texas Gulf coast at Palacios Baptist Encampment. This camp was selected by a group of angry, older people who set out on a mission to find the hottest, most mosquito infested, worst water-tasting portion of earth on God's great globe. When they found Palacios, TX, their mission was finished. Now, before citizens of Palacios start to write me angry letters, I need to add that holy ground does not actually exist. Holy ground is ground made holy because one meets God on it. Every July I met God at Palacios. I first felt God's call to ministry at Palacios. I finally surrendered to that call at Palacios. Some of my greatest memories of my teen-age years were at Palacios. Palacios was to me holy ground, despite its being very hot with many mosquitoes and foul-tasting water.

Church camp had many sacred traditions. Every summer some guy with a lot of hair and shirts made in Hawaii arrived at camp and sang his favorite song or maybe the only song he knew. The song was "Throw Out the Lifeline" about sailors drowning in the sea like lost people dying without having placed their faith in Jesus. Each year this oft-invited singer became very animated during the chorus. He would lean over the pulpit toward the crowd and sling his arms as if he were throwing out a lifeline. With this action, he would sing, "Throoooooooooooow out the lifeline. Throoooooooooooow out the lifeline." One anonymous teen-ager had heard enough. He placed himself in the middle of the center row, about 10 rows from the front. When the colorful singer got to the active part of the song and sang, "Throoooooooooooow out the lifeline." This forever unnamed youth, stood up, grasped his neck as if he had been hooked or hit, and yelled at the top of his voice, "Aahhhhhhhhhhhhhh!" If I remember correctly, the singer never again sang at Palacios Baptist Encampment.

Naughty knees

One more Palacios story: Baptist camps were notorious in past years for their "no-mixed-bathing" rule. I always wondered why they didn't call it the "no-mixed-swimming" rule, since no one I knew was brave enough to bathe together, at least not at church camp. Nevertheless we had the infamous swimming-pool rule. It was written by the same committee that discovered Palacios Encampment. Girls and boys could not swim in the same pool at the same time least they look on one another to lust after each other.

One particular year the rule was amended. Baptists have historically been especially good at this. Some boys had been guilty of getting an early start to the pool for their swimming time, so they could see the girls as they left the pool and walked to their dorms. The new amendment called for all swimmers to wear robes that reached below the knee. This way, no one would be tempted to sin while he or she walked to and from the swimming pool.

Some of us decided to address this subject during the Wednesday afternoon camp talent show. Dressed as females with knees showing, we sang new words to the then familiar show-tune from "South Pacific," entitled, "There is Nothing Like a Dame." Our new words shocked the camp committee as we sang, "There is nothing like a knee. Nothing you can see, that is anything like a knee." Had not my father been on the camp planning committee that year, I feel certain the entire singing group would have been invited to take an early bus ride home.

In all fairness . . . things my mother taught me

Having mentioned my father, in all fairness I need to write something about my mother. Someone sent me these a long time ago. They describe my mother perfectly.

> *My mother taught me:*
> *To appreciate a job well done — "If you're going to kill each other, do it outside. I just finished cleaning."*
> *To value religion — "You had better pray that the stain comes out of the carpet."*
> *To understand sound reason — "Because I said so, that's why!"*
> *To get a grasp of logic — "If you fall out of that tree and break your neck, you're not going to the store with me."*
> *To plan ahead — "Be sure to wear clean underwear in case you're in an accident."*
> *To contemplate osmosis — "Shut your mouth and eat your supper."*
> *To be consistent — "If I've told you once I've told you a million times: Don't exaggerate!"*
> *To anticipate the future — "Just wait 'till we get home."*
> *To explore medical science — "If you don't stop crossing your eyes, they're going to freeze that way."*

To be proud of my roots—"Do you think you were born in a barn?"

To be blessed by justice—"One day you'll have kids. I hope they turn out just like you."

Just when you least expect it

One evening my best friend, Jimmie Don Ulrich, and I were running through the house playing cops and robbers or Cowboys and Indians or some such game. We were making way too much noise and getting on my mother's nerves. Rather than tell us to go outside or just stop running in the house, she hid behind a large chair with one of my plastic guns. As Jimmie Don circled the corner from the hallway into the living room, assured he was well ahead of my pursuit, my dignified, graceful pastor's wife-mother jumped out from behind the chair and yelled, "Pow! Pow! Pow!" He totally collapsed and fell across the den and into the hallway, pretty sure he was really shot. Even though Jimmie Don went on to fly helicopters in Viet Nam, to this day he has flashbacks to a near-death experience that evening in my home as a result of my mother's sense of humor.

See your what?

Thanks to my family, I learned how much fun traveling could be. On one family vacation my mom, dad, Breakfast Bob (my younger brother whose name I will explain later in chapter 9), and I were in El Paso, TX, and decided to walk across the bridge into Juarez, Mexico, so we could say we'd been across the border. Once across the bridge we were approached by one person after another. All offered us some service in return for our money. After enduring this to his wit's end, my dad began to herd us back toward the bridge and the good ole U.S.A. One particular cab driver stayed with us all the way to the bridge offering to show us the city, the mountains, the river, and a host of other sights. When he seemed to be getting nowhere, the frustrated cabbie finally shouted as we approached the bridge, "You want to see my Chihuahua?" Every time that story was repeated at family events, we laughed heartedly. In fact it became kind of an inside family joke. When things would go bad, or an argument would ensue, or we were perplexed, someone would always ask, "You want to see my Chihuahua?" Then one day, I traveled into the western part of Mexico, just south of El Paso, into the Mexican state of . . . you guessed it, Chihuahua. The funniest thing about the story is that we'll never know if the talkative cab driver was offering to show us his state or his dog. Matters not! Fun is wherever you find it.

Called to preach—but not long

Earlier I mentioned being called to the ministry while I was at Palacios Baptist Encampment. I remember calling home to tell my parents the night I surrendered to preach. After a few audible tears from my mother, my father dropped a bomb. He said, "If God has called you to preach, I guess you'd better preach this Sunday night." I returned home from camp on Friday with all day Saturday to prepare my first sermon. I remembered having read a sermon by R.A. Torrey from Daniel 5 on the Feast of Belshazzar. I couldn't get it out of my mind. So, while other novice preachers began their preaching careers in the Gospel of John, I began in the difficult book of Daniel. The sermon was prepared by noon on Saturday.

Then my dad offered a suggestion. "There's no one at the church on Saturday afternoon," he said. "Take the keys and go to the church. Get behind the pulpit. Preach your sermon as if the auditorium was full of people. Do it several times until you are comfortable with your sermon." I did so. Every time I preached my Daniel sermon, it lasted exactly 28 minutes. I was primed, pumped, and ready. I had all the confidence any 17-year-old preacher could hope to have.

Sunday was a long day as I eagerly awaited my turn. Finally the evening service began. A lot of friends were there to hear me preach my inaugural sermon. After the music I walked to the pulpit like I knew what I was doing. I said everything I had planned to say, looked at my watch, and was horrified to discover that my first sermon had lasted seven-and-a-half minutes.

For who's sake?

A few years later, after I gained some experience in preaching, my father decided he could trust me to deliver a sermon longer than seven-and-a-half minutes. He invited me to preach on Sunday morning. I was to fill in for him at the First Baptist Church of Nacogdoches, TX, while he was on vacation. Not only was this a very large church, its morning worship service was broadcast live on a local radio station. This would be my first experience preaching live on the radio. I was so concerned that I do a respectable job with the sermon I forgot to focus on other responsibilities of the morning. When I voiced the offertory prayer, I prayed that we would give in the spirit of the woman who gave all she had. Then—live on deep East Texas radio—I said, "In Jesus name and for HER sake, Amen."

Chapter Two

College Student Daze

During my first week in college I remember thinking how much fun I was having. I believed I was about to have more fun than I had ever had in my lifetime. I was right. Student days are the greatest days of all. New freedoms. New responsibilities. New friends. New surroundings. Life is a daze. And it's great fun. Few students had more fun than I did. Unfortunately my academic transcript reflects just how much fun I had and how much I learned while I was having fun. In fact, to my credit, I never let my studies get in the way of my education.

Take Me Out to the What?

During my senior year in high school I was offered a partial baseball scholarship at a small Baptist college outside of Texas. I had actually completed all of my paperwork to enroll there. However, I forgot to mail the documents. My dad arrived home from a convention and told me he had run into an old friend, Dr. Guy Newman, president of Howard Payne College (now University). He said Dr. Newman wanted to talk to me about my baseball scholarship. Since I had not mailed the official papers to the other school, I was still eligible to talk with Dr. Newman. So my dad and I drove all the way from Houston to Brownwood, TX. We spent the night on one of the top floors of Hotel Brownwood, surely 10 stories taller than the next tallest building in the town. When I awoke the next morning and looked out of the window, I could see forever. Besides the view, I could now breathe without congestion. I had been able to do

25

neither of these growing up in Houston. I was already close to being sold on Howard Payne before ever seeing the campus. Advertised as "the college where everybody is somebody", Howard Payne was a small Baptist school in a small west Texas town. It was everything I had missed during my teen-age years in Houston. As we walked across the campus to the president's office, everyone we saw spoke to us. It was the friendliest place I'd ever been. Once in the president's office, Dr. Newman explained to me that when the Lone Star Conference dropped baseball as a conference sport, Howard Payne had likewise dropped baseball. However, he wanted to re-start the sport. I would be one of a core of players around which this friendly, small-town, small-campus, clean-air school would rebuild its baseball program. When the president offered to give me a partial baseball scholarship, I was hooked. Within days I had all of my paperwork completed and began the pilgrimage toward baseball stardom via Howard Payne College. I enrolled in HPC and graduated in the spring of 1964. Unfortunately I never played for the school's baseball team, because the school never restarted its program. About 25 years after I graduated the school restarted its Yellow Jackets baseball program. I wrote then-president Dr. Don Newberry, who had been a Howard Payne senior when I was a freshman, and shared my story. I offered to at least throw out the first pitch during this historic first season of the new team. Never one to miss a chance to raise a dollar for the old alma mater, Dr. Newberry answered that I ought to first re-pay my baseball scholarship. I never mentioned the issue again. I am, however, the only person I know who accepted a baseball scholarship to a college that did not have a baseball team.

The Klods and pink underwear
    Being a church school and a very conservative one at that,

Howard Payne University allowed no Greek organizations on campus. We thought that was unfair, since those of us who were majoring in religious studies had to take two years of Greek. So, using the Greek alphabet that we had just learned, several of us formed our own, non-university recognized "fraternity." To announce the organization of the Kappa Lambda Omicron Delta Sigma (KLODS) fraternity we all dyed our hair red. This was a lot of fun until the next morning when I awoke to a red pillow case. Not wanting to upset my mother on the next trip home, I put the bright red pillow case in the washing machine with all my other white undergarments. An hour later I had pink underwear, pink undershirts, pink socks, and pink handkerchiefs. My mother had always told me to be sure I had on clean underwear when I went out in case I had a wreck. I wasn't sure if two pair of pink undershorts would help much at the emergency room.

Will you open?

My freshman year of college included an enormous amount of time spent playing 42 with friends in the dorm. We played so much 42 that once at a church meeting when time came for the opening prayer, a domino friend of mine was asked; "Will you open us?" His reply was "Sure, I bid 42, no-low with doubles as a suit of their own." I stopped laughing when I realized that he and I were the only ones who thought it was funny.

What did you say was in my sandwich?

My roommate my freshman year was an agriculture major from "out of Lometa, TX." Considering Lometa had only one blinking light, almost everything there was "out of Lometa." However, he lived so far out no one passed his house on the way to town. He would go home every weekend and return with a large bag of sandwiches. Since the college dining room was closed on Sunday nights and local churches served only finger food (food the size of your little finger), I devoured those "out of Lometa" sandwiches week after week. In the spring I finally went home with my roomie. No electricity. No running water. No cows. I was a bit confused since he had pictures of cows on the wall over his bed. I finally asked, "Those sandwiches I've been eating on Sunday nights . . .?" "Goat meat" he replied gleefully. "We raise goats" he said. I choked a bit and gave thanks it wasn't worse. Since my roomie was transferring at the end of the semester, I began to pray for a new roommate—one whose family raised cows.

The discipline of replacement

Building the homecoming bonfire was a great freshman tradition. Placing an outhouse on the top was the highlight. The guys in my freshman class topped off our bonfire with a deluxe two-seater outhouse. We were so proud of our accomplishment that we called the newspaper to take a picture. The next day our diligent work was rewarded with a front-page photo in *The Brownwood Bulletin*. However, before the day was over, we were invited to the president's office. Unfortunately the owner of the outhouse had recognized his missing two-seater when he saw the newspaper's photo. Ever tried to return a badly burned outhouse to its original and upright position?

Matthew's Christmas tree

Christmas was a special time on campus. Not willing to wait until we could go home to enjoy a Christmas tree, some of us went looking for a nice tree. We found one growing in and out of a rural cemetery. The tree's roots were inside the fence, but since the majority of the tree was outside of the fence, we felt justified in cutting it and hauling it to our dorm room. The next day some angel hair unexpectedly appeared on our tree. A friend had "borrowed it" from the dorm director's tree in the dorm lobby. Very soon the dorm director arrived looking for the missing angel hair. We survived that scare and enjoyed our tree, minus angel hair.

When we returned from the Christmas holidays we were surprised to find our unwatered tree extremely dry. In a late-night discussion the question was posed as to whether dry Christmas trees would burn. To find an answer one student lit a match and set it to the tree. Immediately the tree went up in a ball of fire. Not willing to burn our dorm room, we grabbed the burning tree and rushed it across the hall to the shower room. However when the shower was turned on, the tree's flames turned to black smoke and made a nasty stain on the heretofore white shower walls. Our dorm had an elderly black janitor named Matthew. Matthew had only one tooth left in his head. The tooth was hanging on a thin thread as were his nerves the morning after the tree fire. Early that morning we were awakened with heavy banging on our door and loud cursing. Matthew was saying something about a smoked and stained shower stall and a dead, burned Christmas tree nearby.

Not long after that Matthew died. We planted the tree in his memory. That's when we learned that while dead Christmas trees will burn, they will not grow

An odor that was not funny

One day we went hunting. None of us was a very good hunter. We didn't know enough to stop to check what was in season. We just took a gun and went out into the country and started to look for some varmints to shoot. Something jumped and ran in front of us. The one with the gun whirled and shot. The white, furry animal slumped over. As we were celebrating our kill—of what we assumed was a rabbit—we began to smell an awful odor. We had shot a rare, albino skunk. What do you do with an albino skunk? Maybe it was so rare it was worth something. So we picked up the dead skunk and placed it carefully in a box in the trunk of our car. The closer we got to town, the stronger the smell seemed to become. "You sure that skunk was dead?" asked one member of the hunting party. We took the maybe-dead-maybe-not-dead skunk to a local animal doctor. He obviously smelled it before we entered his office, because he started yelling something about getting the skunk out of there. So we drove back to the country and disposed of the skunk. Back at the dorm we showered and went to dinner in the dining hall. Funny, but no one would sit near us that night . . . or breakfast the next morning . . . or lunch.

Toilet paper, chicken wire and $50

One of the best collegiate activities is the building of parade floats. I participated in a series of homecoming float constructions. The one that is strongest in my memory is a float prepared for a Democracy-in-Action Week. The 1960s were years of conflict with the Soviet Union. Our quasi-fraternity (KLODS) planned a float with the cross made out of chicken wire and stuffed with white toilet tissue, a hammer and sickle cut out of plywood and painted red, and a young boy facing the cross with his back to the hammer and sickle. The sides of the float were to be wrapped with chicken wire and stuffed with multi-colored toilet tissue. The school gave us $50 for construction supplies with the stipulation that we had to enter the parade or return the $50. We worked long and diligently into far too many late nights for our grade-point average to endure. On the Saturday morning of the parade a 40-mile-per-hour wind was gusting through Brownwood. When we pulled out of the barn with the trailer containing the float, the wind immediately re-distributed all the toilet paper down the road. The parents of the little boy decided riding on the float in the wind was too dangerous for him. We were left with a trailer wrapped in chicken wire, a chicken-wire cross, no little boy, and a large, strong, red, plywood hammer and sickle. Not wanting to lose the $50 construction grant, we decided to enter the parade anyway. I was in the car pulling the trailer and listening to a Brownwood radio do a live broadcast of the parade: "Following the Brownwood High School band we have a nice . . . it appears to be a float signifying . . . there is a communist hammer and cycle . . . there's a lot of chicken wire . . . and here comes the Comanche High School Band." We got to keep our $50 and our pride. Of course we weren't allowed in any more parades.

Radio humor

Speaking of Brownwood radio, the town actually was well known for one of its radio stations, located "just a stone's throw from Howard Payne College." Some students who shall forever remain nameless checked on this one night and actually were able to throw some stones all the way to the radio station. We had one TV set in the dorm lobby, but we had no cable or antenna, so we could receive only snow. As an alternative we listened to the radio. One night the Brownwood weather forecaster said, "The low tonight will be near tomorrow." That made sense.

Late at night the local programming gave way to a powerful station out of Cuidad Acuna, Coahuila, Mexico, just across the border from Del Rio, TX. Most of its programming was devoted to faith-healers. One night a faith-healer said, "If you want to be healed, place one hand on your Bible, the other on your radio, and raise the other one." Now there's a listener that needed healing!

The best sound we ever heard on a Brownwood radio station came from classmates Ray Hilderbrand and Jill Jackson, better known as "Paul and Paula", singing what was to become their million-seller, "Hey, Hey Paula." After touring England, appearing on the Ed Sullivan Show, American Bandstand, and various other venues, Ray returned to Howard Payne to finish his degree. He was the only celebrity to ever play on our intramural basketball team, the Klods. Even with Ray, the Klod games never were on the radio.

Turn over in your Bible to . . .

One of my college roommates who shall forever remain nameless did not date very often. He did try to get a date, but just got turned down a lot. One girl excused herself from dating him when she used the classic excuse: "A previous engagement just came up." He could dial only half a phone number and someone would answer and say, "No." When he did get a date, he became so nervous that the evening was ruined. The non-experienced student was introduced to 1 John 4:18 which says (in the only translation we had back then, *The King James*), *There is no fear in love; but perfect love casteth out fear.* He was excited and said that on his next date, he was going to read that to the girl. That date likewise ended in disaster. When he opened his Bible to read, he got confused. Turning to John 4:18 instead of 1 John 4:18, he read to his date the following words: *"For thou hast had five husbands and he whom thou now hast is not thine husband."*

Term-paper tips

Professor Russell Bowers, a seminary faculty colleague, compiled a list of helpful suggestions that I sure could have used when I was in college. Seems he grew weary of grading papers with grammatical errors in them, so he assisted his students with the following suggestions:

Avoid run on sentences they are hard to read.
About sentence fragments.
Avoid awkward, affected, alliteration.
Don't use no double negatives.
Avoid commas, that aren't necessary.
Verbs has to agree with their subjects.

Likewise, pronouns have to agree with its referents.
Never use a long word when a miniscule one will do.
Kill all exclamation marks!!!!!!!
Who needs rhetorical questions?
Never, under any circumstances, use repetitive, repetitious
* redundancies.*
Prepositions are not words to end sentences with.
Parenthetical remarks (however relevant) are unnecessary.
Remember to never split an infinitive.
One should never generalize.
Be more or less specific.
Even if a mixed-metaphor sings, it should be derailed.
Avoid clichés like the plague (they are old hat).

Sermons were getting weaker by the week

I did get to preach occasionally during my first three years at Howard Payne. Then in the spring semester of my third year I was invited to preach at the Union Baptist Church in Pontotoc, TX. Actually a lot of ministerial students preached there, including several of my preacher buddies. Tradition called for the visiting student-preacher not to tell the next student-preacher what would happen. The church invited me to preach on a given Sunday. I did so. After the service I noticed a small group of members meeting in the back corner of the auditorium. Then one of them came over to me and said, "Uh, do you suppose you could come back next Sunday?" This happened for nine straight Sundays. Then one Sunday the small group met briefly and disbursed to their pickup trucks. No one invited me back. My time at Pontotoc was over. I guess my sermons were getting weaker by the week. Maybe that's why the lady told me, "Oh, Brother Dan, every sermon you preach is better than the next one." Hummmm! What I never figured out was how they knew that I only had nine sermons.

Chapter Three

Student Pastorates

I truly believe a special subdivision of heaven is reserved for folks who spent their lives as members of small churches served by student pastors. They endured a series of short-term weekend warriors and listened to many a wannabee preacher deliver sermons borrowed from books, professors, and chapel speakers and based on theology-in-the-making. I'm not sure what kind of mansions these longsuffering church members will have, but I do believe they will spend eternity listening to the best preaching from heaven's greatest preachers. I did my time in a series of small churches as I persecuted the saints but put absolutely no fear in Satan. I did, however, learn valuable lessons.

When Billy Jack blows his horn

One summer I served as a substitute pastor at the church in which a friend was pastor, I subbed for him while he served as a student summer missionary. As it happens in most Texas rural communities, a revival meeting was planned for the third week of August. I was told about Billy Jack, the community agnostic who had said he would never enter the church building again. It was more of a dare than an item of information. It's a rural church game called, "Let's-See-if-the-New-Guy-Can-Reach-the-Community-Agnostic." Well, I've always liked challenges, so I set about to meet Billy Jack. He actually admitted to me that he'd like to see what was going on at the church, but he had made a statement of never again entering the church building and was a man of his word.

Behind the church building, like in many rural communities, stood an old brush arbor, a tabernacle of sorts. I suggested to the church that we hold our revival meetings outside—momentarily forgetting what outside in Texas was like in August. Before I could regain my senses, the church had voted to do this. So as not to appear totally incompetent, I then convinced Billy Jack that he could attend the revival meeting since it was not technically inside the church building. We agreed on a compromise. If we'd leave the outside flaps on the tabernacle open, he'd drive his pick-up truck underneath, close enough to hear the music and sermon. To the absolute amazement of everyone, Billy Jack attended the second service of the revival meeting. With me on the verge of becoming a community legend, a terrible thing happened. Not being accustomed to such activities, Billy Jack fell asleep during the sermon. Toward the end of the sermon he fell forward and hit his head on the pickup truck's horn. The horn echoed against the metal side flaps of the tabernacle and made a rather loud noise. In fact the noise was so loud it woke up six sleeping babies . . . and two deacons. Two people rushed to the altar because they thought Gabriel was near.

Paying the Preacher

During my senior year at Howard Payne University a pulpit committee—the forerunner of a pastor-search committee—asked if I would preach in "lieu" of a call at their church. Understanding that they really meant in "view" of a call, I agreed. After the sermon they voted to call me as the pastor of the Robinson Springs Baptist Church situated half way between DeLeon and Desdemona, TX. The church was at the intersection of two gravel roads. No houses were visible from any side of the small church building. They had an interesting practice on Sunday evenings. Late on Sunday afternoon the family I happened to be eating dinner with that day would say, "Well,

Preacher, it's about time to get on down to the church. You go ahead. We'll be seeing you." I would go to the church, park my car, go inside, and sit on the front row looking over my sermon notes for the evening. On many Sunday nights, I would hear vehicles enter the church's small parking lot, car doors open and close, and vehicles leave. No one ventured inside. After I was convinced that no one was planning on attending the evening service, I would lock the church door, go to my car, and see what was in the back seat—canned vegetables, smoked meat, cake, pie, cookies, etc. This was their way of "paying" the preacher . . . and not having to attend church on Sunday evening. As I look back on some of those early sermon notes, I have decided I was overpaid.

Label-less and disbanded

Joanne and I married shortly after my graduation from Howard Payne and while I was still pastor at Robinson Springs. The good folks there were so accustomed to paying the preacher with food they gave us an old-fashioned canned-goods wedding pounding . . . and removed the labels from all the cans. It made for some interesting early-marriage meals. When I read my pastoral resignation to the church, one of the two remaining deacons amended it to disband the church. I didn't know a church could do that. But they explained to me that before they called me as pastor, they had had a lengthy discussion as to whether to continue or disband. Most of the members had moved into nearby towns and continued to return to Robinson Springs on Sunday only because it had been their families' church. A division of opinions occurred at that discussion. Their compromise was to call one more preacher from Howard Payne University. When he resigned, they would disband. Or, at least that's what they told me. Twenty-five years later, when I stood in front of my Church Growth Evangelism classes at

Southwestern Baptist Seminary, I would explain to them that I was well qualified to teach the subject since my first church had disbanded on my resignation. The puzzled expressions on the faces of the students were better than all the food in those label-less cans.

Well-side manners

I enjoyed visiting with one rather poor family in the church. Not only did their food always seem to taste better, but their ice tea was the best I'd ever had. On a hot summer Sunday afternoon I'd consume a quart jar of it at one setting. One afternoon my host invited me into the back yard to look down in the well for some reason I've long-forgotten. As I leaned over to look in the well, my arm brushed against a rather large cow chip, as I knocked it into the well. I've put a lot of thought into how that cow chip got up on the well ledge. All I really know is that their ice tea never tasted good again.

Mt. Pisgah's not so lofty height

One of the most popular hymns during these seminary days was "Sweet Hour of Prayer". It includes a line that speaks of "Mount Pisgah's lofty height"—a reference to the mountain whose heights Moses twice ascended to view the Promised Land. Having resigned at the now-disbanded Robinson Springs Baptist Church, I became pastor of the Mount Pisgah Baptist Church. I first, of course, obtained a guarantee that the church would not disband upon my resignation. Mount Pisgah was situated in the Brushy Creek community between Palestine and Frankston, TX. Just for the record, during my 18 months there I never saw a creek, a peak, or the Promised Land. That pastorate did, however, provide several mountain-top experiences.

Still a Methodist nose

One of the great experiences at Brushy Creek was conducting my first baptismal service. Actually it was my second, since in the pastoral ministry class at seminary we had practiced baptizing each other. The practice round should not count, however, since my baptismal candidate was six-foot-four-inches tall and I banged his head against the wall of the six-foot classroom baptistery. Now this was winter in East Texas. The church at Brushy Creek had no baptistery. The weather was too cold to baptize in the stock tanks, so we borrowed the baptistery at the First Baptist Church in Frankston and held an afternoon service. We had no robes, so the middle-aged lady whom I was to baptize simply wore a full cotton dress. She was a Methodist who had married a member of our church. I did as I had been taught at seminary. I assured her that she needed to be baptized again.

The baptismal pool at Frankston had a glass front from top to bottom. Those seated in the auditorium could see the entire proceedings in the baptismal pool. As I began to recline the candidate in the pool, the water began to swirl. She panicked. Waving her hands to keep her dress from rising with the air bubbles only caused the water to swirl more. The more I tried to get her under the water, the more she stirred the water in a futile attempt to keep her dress down. Best I could tell, the candidate still had a Methodist nose since I gave up before getting it under the water. Of course, with the glass front, the entire audience watched this spectacle. My faithful church members were laughing so hard that our pianist, Mrs. Gatlin, though seated at the piano, forgot to play "Up From the Grave He Arose."

An unwanted guest

Despite her momentary lapse of memory at the baptism service, Mrs. Gatlin was a Brushy Creek saint. Every Sunday morning in the winter months this long-time believer, now alone in the world, would drive to the church an hour before Sunday School to turn on the heaters so the building would be warm when the members arrived. While she waited, she rehearsed on the piano the hymns of the morning. Mrs. Gatlin was a faithful church pianist. She played every hymn in four/four time, but she was faithful.

One winter Sunday she was met by a small group of folks from the Midway community, a few miles down the farm-to-market road. Their church had been without a pastor for more than a year. It had ceased meeting. Now its members wanted to start meeting again. They wondered if some of our members could help them in this re-start. Mrs. Gatlin quickly volunteered me to preach there early every Sunday morning before our services began. I countered by volunteering her to play the piano. So early the next Sunday we went to Midway, where we found a small group of people eagerly awaiting our arrival. The Midway church building was extremely cold from too many winter Sundays with no occupants. As I introduced the first hymn—while still wearing my overcoat—frost poured from my mouth. Mrs. Gatlin played the prelude; then we began to sing. To keep the piano from ruining, the Midway members had left a light bulb burning inside it. The warmth of the light bulb had attracted one of God's creatures. He was obviously not pleased with our music and especially with Mrs. Gatlin's piano playing. During the third verse I heard a loud, blood-curdling scream from the direction of the piano. I looked over in time to see crawling across Mrs. Gatlin's shoes the biggest, longest, blackest, snake I'd ever seen. I'm not absolutely sure, but I think when Mrs. Gatlin went by me, she was humming, "Pass Me Not, O Gentle Savior."

Better buried, than propped up
     One of the most traumatic times in the life of a young min-

ister is when that first call occurs about the death of a church member. At that moment he knows a funeral service must be planned. "When did we cover this in the pastoral-ministry class?" is the immediate question. One small-town funeral director told me he had trained more young ministers in how to conduct funerals than any seminary had ever done. I don't know if he was correct, but I suddenly felt helpless when the news of my first funeral service arrived. I had seen the deceased man only a few times. I wasn't sure I'd recognize the body, so I decided to go by his home first before going to the funeral home. I thought maybe I'd see a picture on the mantle that would remind me whose funeral service I was about to perform. As I pulled into the driveway, I was surprised by how many cars and trucks were there. Wasn't anyone at the funeral home? Entering the living room I suddenly understood why no one was at the funeral home. I also realized that I no longer had to wonder what the deceased looked like! There in the living room, where the couch used to be, was the casket. Inside propped up was the deceased. That's when I was introduced to the East Texas custom of "setting up with the body." So we sat there in the living room discussing the desires of the family for the funeral service. Maybe it was just me, but I kept expecting the deceased to offer his suggestions. I was the happiest young preacher in the world when the family decided on a closed-casket funeral.

The real pastor

I often tell my seminary students who are preparing to be pastors that just because a church bestows that title on them does not mean they are thereby the real pastor of the church. Always some person, family, or small group of people really serves as pastor, especially in small, rural churches. The best way to discover this real pastor is to observe very carefully at the church business meeting. The people will all look at the same person before they cast their votes. That's the real pastor. I learned this at Brushy Creek. His name was E. B. Birdwell. He was a saint. No young pastor could have wished for a more supportive deacon. Mr. Birdwell taught the adult Sunday-school class in the church auditorium. When he finished (but not before), we began the worship service. One Sunday the lesson was from the Old Testament prophet *Habakkuk*. Mr. Birdwell kept mispronouncing the name and calling him *HABA-cuk*. He ran the first two syllables together and placed heavy emphasis on the last syllable, instead of *Ha-BAK-uck*, with emphasis on the middle syllable, like they taught at seminary. Once I offered a correction but quickly withdrew it when everyone turned and stared at me like I had just committed the unpardonable sin. I may have been the pastor, but E. B. Birdwell was the resident Bible scholar—the real pastor. Come to think of it, the word may be pronounced *HABA-cuk*.

Let us spray!

My friend and former faculty colleague Justice Anderson shared the following story with me from his seminary student-pastor days:

"While pastor of a county-seat church in Southeast Texas, I invited a colleague to visit and lead us in an old-fashioned, 10-day revival meeting. We both were commuting to Fort Worth twice a week to attend our doctoral seminars. The meeting was during the summer and drew fairly large crowds. We had worked diligently to have maximum attendance the last Sunday morning. We had invited several prospective church members and were expecting a good response to our evangelistic invitation. That Sunday morning was warm. Our church at that time had no air-conditioning. We did have large, screen doors on the entrance side of the auditorium. We opened these on warm days in order to catch the morning breeze.

"The auditorium was full and the screen doors loosely opened when the meeting began. The preacher delivered a stirring evangelistic message, then began to offer the altar call. While the audience sang, I as pastor stood at the front while the evangelist urged the people to respond. Suddenly, I observed a stir in the audience close to the screen doors. The stir seemed to move across the auditorium. Elderly women who could hardly climb the steps suddenly jumped up on the pews. I then saw what was happening. A tranquil skunk had leisurely strolled through the screen doors and was moving across the auditorium under the pews. I immediately stopped the music, ran to close the door to the children's nursery, and declared the service dismissed as people were shouting and moving about to direct the skunk out the back door. One overly enthusiastic deacon threw a song book at the intruder but fortunately missed. Finally, the polecat was driven out the back door, only to be executed by a neighbor's shotgun.

"The poor evangelist-seminary student gained undesired fame from the incident. 'Why, he can even attract skunks with his invitational procedures.' One of my deacons congratulated me for not dismissing the service with the traditional 'Let us pray' — he said the skunk might have thought I said, 'Let us spray!' A local correspondent sent in a report which appeared on the front page of newspapers in Dallas and Houston. It was entitled, 'From pew to pew the *scenter* went.' Thank goodness the devilish skunk decided to retain his spray."

Into my what?

Another friend of mine decided much too early in his ministry that he was ready to preach his first sermon in Spanish. He did well through the sermon, since he had practiced extensively. However, he should have left the invitation to the Spanish-speaking host pastor. Confusing the Spanish word for heart—*corazon*—with the Spanish word for shorts—*calzones* (often used to refer to undershorts or underwear), my friend passionately exclaimed to his attentive audience, "Jesus died for you, and tonight He wants to come into your undershorts." Unfazed by the confusion on their faces, he continued, "Yes, my friend, tonight you can invite Jesus into your undershorts. Many friends are praying for you to surrender your undershorts to the Lord tonight. Just step out into the aisle and move to the front, take this wonderful pastor by the hand, and let him help you invite Jesus into your undershorts." Fortunately, to avoid further disaster the pastor took over the invitation at that point. However, church members went away having attended a service they would never forget.

Chapter Four

Theology and Practice

I completed a 98-hour graduate degree in two-and-a-half years while I served as pastor of a church. Even though Southwestern Baptist Seminary was situated in Fort Worth, we never lived in Fort Worth. I commuted to seminary in a carpool the entire time. Not smart! Certainly no laughing matter! Yet times of genuine humor occurred as Joanne and I struggled our way through these early years of our marriage and our seminary student years. We often felt like praying the prayer of another student who, when called on to pray in class one day, prayed, "Lord, bless our professor and our class, and take care of Yourself, because if anything happens to You, we're all in a lot of trouble. Amen."

Beginning Seminary in a Bug

For my first year of seminary studies I commuted 80 miles round trip from Irving, TX, in a Volkswagen bug with Roy Epperson, Jan Daehnert, and Carroll Duke. We were a fearsome foursome. Most of the controversial issues in theology were solved in that VW bug somewhere between Fort Worth and Irving. One day during final exams the VW surrendered to the heavy weight of systematic theology and philosophy of religion. Somewhere in the Mid-Cities area, the loyal carrier just quit. I don't even remember how we traveled the remainder of the journey that day, but I do remember sitting in a final exam, as I grieved over a faithful friend.

Three planted, but no one watered

Three of the above-mentioned foursome lived in the same Irving apartment complex. With no classes on Mondays we had discussed how to best spend our free day. We agreed that we needed physical exercise. Adjacent to our apartments was a piece of land that once had been a garden. Roy Epperson made a visit to the woman who owned the land. She said she would be happy for us to plant a garden on her late husband's land. So early one Monday morning we made a trip to the garden store. With not enough combined knowledge of gardening to grow Johnson grass, we bought everything we thought might possibly grow. Then we stopped by the rental place to rent a rototiller. All day that Monday we broke ground, pulled weeds, moved rocks, and planted seeds. At the end of the day we stood beside our work; we were proud but pooped.

I remember the next morning as one of the worst days of my life. I could not move the muscles I knew I had, not to mention the new muscles I had discovered during the last 24 hours. About mid morning I made it to the front door and looked out to learn that none of us had gone to seminary that day. In the next few days I learned something about my body—if it worked, it hurt. I never wanted to see that garden again, much less water it and pull weeds. Several weeks later our garden produced its harvest —a medium-size bag of somewhat dry green beans.

The carpool shift

By my last year and a half in seminary I had moved and joined another car pool. This group did not solve as many theological issues as my earlier group had, but we did have our share of discussions. Not being as homogeneous we also had our share of arguments. In fact the Southern Baptist Conservative Resurgence may well have started in that carpool. As I think about it, if we could have gotten that same carpool together for an hour and a half, we might have solved the theological controversies that necessitated a resurgence. One afternoon as we sped down the highway, the student who was seated behind the driver got a little too critical of the driver. The driver said, "You want to drive? Come on, drive!" and proceeded to move to the right side of the front seat. The front-seat rider quickly dove into the back seat and I moved from the right side of the back seat to the left as the chief critic climbed over the seat and behind the wheel. When we stopped laughing at the absurdity of it all, we concluded that God must have something special for the four of us to do, because we should have all been killed in that car-pool stunt.

Talking through the turn

Billie Hanks took his turn to drive the seminary carpool. He arrived in a nice, new car. The smell of the new leather and the unaccustomed quietness of the ride caused the rest of us to sleep even more soundly than normal during our one-hour commute to Fort Worth. That morning Billie had also brought along a new Christian to show him the seminary. Billie talked non-stop for the duration of the trip. So intense was this conversation that Billie went the wrong way at the Hillsboro Y on Interstate 35. Taking the right lane instead of the left lane, we headed further away from Fort Worth toward Dallas. Like a commuter-train rider awakes just before his stop, I awoke about the time we should have been arriving on the south edge of Fort Worth, but the surroundings were unfamiliar. Then I recognized a few buildings. I woke up Ron Durham, who was sleeping in the back seat beside me. I don't remember what Ron said, but I had just missed an 8 a.m. evangelism exam and was not very happy. "Billie! You idiot!" I yelled in Christian love, "We're in downtown Dallas!" Since then Billie has traveled all over the world, but I'm confident he has never been in downtown Dallas without hearing my voice.

Three Legendary Stories

All institutions have a collection of legends that are repeated for each new generation. Around Southwestern the story is told about a professor who went to his classroom early to drop off his coat and hat before he went to his office. When he did not return by 10 minutes after the scheduled start time of the class, the students left. The next day the students arrived in class to meet a furious professor. "How dare you leave my classroom before I arrive? Did you not see my hat on the desk? When my hat is here; I am here and don't you forget it!" The next day the professor arrived to see hats on every desk in the room but no students.

A well-known missions professor had a practice of taking a nap in the faculty lounge each day following lunch. When all the other professors had finished eating and returned to their office, this professor would carefully take off his slacks and fold them over the back of a chair and lie down on the couch. One day as he was napping, the wife of the seminary president entered the room with a tour group of women from her church. There on the couch was the distinguished professor in his underwear. At the next faulty meeting a motion was made barring women from the faculty lounge except for social occasions, which this definitely was not.

So many alumni have claimed to be the student in this next story that true identity is impossible. As a professor lectured, a student slept. Another student seated next to the sleeping one leaned over and whispered; "The professor just called on you to pray." Startled, the future minister became full awake, stood to his feet, and started to pray. After a rather long prayer, the student said "Amen" and sat down. To this the professor responded, "Bro. So-in-so, if you have caught up on your prayer life, I'd like to continue my lecture." This story reminds me of the student who was asked to lead a time of prayer after a tragedy had befallen the seminary family. He began with, "Let us bow our heads in a moment of silent prayer for 30 seconds."

Ice-cream honorarium

Jack Terry shared another legendary story from the seminary's School of Religious Education: "Dr. J.M. Price was known to be extremely frugal. While dean of the School of Religious Education, he asked five of the leading religious educators in the world—who were of course on his faculty—to do an educational conference for him at his church in Rendon, TX. He invited Dr. Joe Davis Heacock, who would follow him as dean of the School of Religious Education for 17 years; Dr. W. L. Howse, who would become the Sunday School Secretary at the Baptist Sunday School Board; Dr. Lee McCoy, who was the leading writer in religious educational administration in the world; Dr. Philip Harris, who would later become the director for Church Training Program at the Baptist Sunday School Board; and Dr. Ann Bradford, who would become world recognized as the founder of Southern Baptist kindergarten work; to lead age-group conferences for him. The team rode to the church each evening in Dr. Price's automobile. For five long nights these five taught and ministered to the Sunday-school workers in his church. On the last night the five were discussing what they thought Dr. Price would give them for an honorarium. On the way home that evening Dr. Price stopped at an ice-cream parlor and bought each team member a one-scoop ice-cream cone. When they got back in the car he said to them, 'The ice cream cone is your honorarium for the week; I really believe you have all been overpaid!'"

Old-fashioned professors

A few seminary students seemed to delight in trapping a professor with an off-the-wall question. I remember a lecture on heaven that was interrupted by a student who asked, "Professor, I'm worried. How will I be able to get my white robe on over my wings in heaven?" The professor, without blinking an eye, replied, "Son, that won't be your problem. You need to worry about getting your pants on over your tail." Another professor well advanced in age was asked by a young student, "Professor, how old do you have to be before you stop being tempted by women?" I don't rightly know," said the professor. "You probably ought to ask someone older than me." They don't make professors like they used to.

Baptism and tongues

Pastoral ministry classes were especially helpful and so very practical. I remember the day we practiced baptizing. We used a chapel that is no longer on campus. The chapel had a baptistery where wannabee preachers could practice on each other. It was a very small baptistery—after more than 20 interim pastorates, I can easily say this baptistry was the smallest I've even been in. I've been in a few baptisteries. After the professor demonstrated the proper way to baptize, we drew names for baptismal partners. I only had one problem. My partner was six-foot-four inches and the baptistery was only six-feet long. After I banged his head on the wall, I think he was speaking in tongues.

Borrowed from Another Book: Money Changing

One of my colleagues, Al Fasol, has written a book of humor entitled, *Humor with a Halo: True Funny Stories from Church Life*. Al's book contains a chapter titled, "The Quaint Humor on a Seminary Campus." With his permission, I share the following stories from his book:

"Faculty lounges are notoriously bad places for colleagues to seek sympathy for mundane problems, or to receive affirmation if the colleague seems to be a little pleased with self. A theology professor strolled into the faculty lounge at noon one day and interrupted conversations with a request: 'Can anyone break this five-dollar bill?' 'I can,' said the archeology professor. The theology professor handed the five-dollar bill to the archaeology professor who tore it in two, handed the pieces back to the owner, and resumed his conversation."[1]

Borrowed from another book: physical fitness

In yet another story borrowed from, *Humor with a Halo: True Funny Stories from Church Life:*

"An Old Testament professor was notoriously against physical exercise. Frequently, he would quote Bernard Baruch: 'I get my exercise being pall bearer for people who exercise.' Just as frequently he would say, 'If you ever see me running, look to see what's chasing me.' A preaching professor and an ethics professor made an effort to persuade the Old Testament professor that exercise is good for one's health. Said the preaching professor, 'I walk two miles every night and as a result my resting heartbeat is 52 beats per minute.' Rather than being impressed, the Old Testament professor responded, in mock alarm, 'Fifty-two beats a minute. Why, man, your tombstone will say you were dead a long time before you knew it!' Several months later, the ethics professor, on his first day back on campus after undergoing open heart surgery, determinedly sought the Old Testament professor. He found him in the faculty lounge, marched gingerly over to him and said, 'My doctor said that if I had not exercised, I would be dead right now.' Undaunted, the Old Testament professor smiled and said, 'Now that you have had your surgery, you will probably live as long as I do.'"[2]

Student change-of-grade request form

One seminary professor became so irritated with students wanting a higher grade at the end of the semester, he developed (or copied) a form for students to complete so he would not have to meet with them and hear their reasoning for a grade change. Here is his change of grade request form:

Should you receive a grade for this class with which you are not satisfied, please feel free to complete this "Student Change-of-Grade Request Form."

Name of course_____

Name of professor_____

Grade I received_____

Grade I should have received:_____A+____

My grade should be raised for the following reason:

_____ There must be a mistake somewhere.

_____ I was not well at the times of the exams.

_____ My mind always goes blank during times of examination.

_____ This grade ruined my chance of getting a scholarship

_____ This grade ruined my perfect A+ average.

_____ This grade alone will keep me out of the doctoral program.

_____ This is the only bad grade I've ever made since pre-school.

_____ This grade grieved my parents whose pride I am.

_____ Conditions in the classroom were not conducive to concentration.

_____ I have to work, therefore I should be given extra points.

_____ I am married therefore I should be given a break.

_____ I am single therefore I should be given a break.

_____ I would have done better if I had taken the exam given to last semester's class.

_____ Several around me copied from my exam yet made higher grades than I did.

_____ Some who did not work as hard as I did got a better grade.

_____ At any point of the semester, one of my grandparents was ill.

_____ The exam questions were ambiguous. Therefore I should be graded according to my interpretations of the questions.

_____ Some exam questions were matters of opinion and I should not be graded down because my opinion is deemed to be incorrect.

_____ I studied this subject from a broad philosophical viewpoint therefore I was unable to answer the technical-based questions.

_____ I am philosophically oriented to the realm of ideas. I respond to the sweep and scope of great intellects. My work is beyond the interest in petty details and parrot-like memorizing of those who are merely students.

_____ At the time of the exam I was suffering from a severe case of cognitive dissonance and was incapable of coping with the stress of the hour.

_____ It is not a higher grade I seek. I care nothing about grades. I think grades are wicked and I disapprove of them. However, this pernicious system of which I am a victim requires grades for achieving success and therefore, I seek a higher grade.

_____ I will continue to harass you until you raise my grade, so make it easy on yourself. Remember, "If you strike a tree enough times, it will fall."

_____ My intentions are to graduate and become a trustee of this institution. You will be prouder of me if you raise my grade now.

Return this form to hahahahahahahaha@swbts.edu.

Walking to Jerusalem

To finish a 98-hour degree in two-and-a-half years I had to complete my Hebrew requirement at another institution. With permission of the academic dean, I took a summer course in Modern Conversational Hebrew at the University of Texas. The events of the first day should have alerted me to how tough this class was going to be. When the Professor asked how many already knew the Hebrew alphabet, 20 hands out of 23 students in the class went up. All 20 were Jewish hands. Among the three Gentiles in the class, the other two were girls who were engaged to Jewish guys. The teacher exclaimed, "Good! We'll go straight to vocabulary."

The format of the class beginning with the second day was 90 minutes of instruction during which English could be spoken, then 90 minutes of class during which no English could be spoken. I was so far behind at the start I could never catch up in six weeks. But I gave it the old college try. Needing a 70 average to pass the course, I finished with a 69 and three-fifths. Rounded off, it was the hardest "D" I ever made. I was never prouder of an "A." My best day of the six-week course was the day the professor asked me, in Hebrew, if I had ever been to Jerusalem. I answered in my best Hebrew, but I got the wrong verb and the class broke out in laughter. The Professor said, "Mr. Crawford, you may be the only person in this class who believes the New Testament, but you will not *walk* on the water to Jerusalem."

[1] Al Fasol, *Humor with a Halo: True Funny Stories From Church Life*. (Lima, Ohio: G.S. Publishing Co. 1989), p. 76.

[2] Ibid, pp. 76-77.

Chapter Five

Young Once, Immature Forever

On our first date, my eventual wife-to-be, Joanne, informed me that God had told her she would marry a Baptist student director. Ordinarily that would have ended our dating relationship. I had friends who were involved in our college BSU (Baptist Student Union, as we called it back then). I thought they were entirely too spiritual. I was not into early-morning prayer meetings and late-night Bible studies. I was, however, connected to the BSU. I was on their Top 10 prayer list. To make a long story short, Joanne and I dated, got engaged, married, and on seminary graduation, I entered collegiate ministry. Since I was unsure exactly what God wanted me to do in the way of ministry, this provided a good opportunity to be involved in many different phases of ministry—all wrapped up in one job. Plus, it saved my marriage. When God speaks to Joanne, I plan accordingly. So I spent 15 wonderful years ministering on three university campuses. Then one night I fell asleep during an all-night lock-in and knew my days in collegiate ministry were numbered. You can't be young forever, but you can be immature for many years.

Go where, with us?

My first assignment in collegiate ministry was to Pan American University (now the University of Texas at Pan American) situated on the U.S.-Mexican border. Seventy-five percent of the student body spoke Spanish as its first language. Over 90 percent of our town had Spanish surnames. So what better way to publicize the mid-winter retreat to Horsetail Falls, Mexico, than to advertise in Spanish. After all, I had passed Spanish in high school. So I designed a beautiful brochure and on the front proclaimed in bold letters. *"Vamos a la cola de caballo!"* Meaning to announce we were going to Horsetail Falls, I had literally announced we were going to the tail of the horse.

A Spanish-Jewish diet

Part of my responsibility at Pan American University was to teach credit Bible courses in the Bible Chair program of the school. Naturally my classes were composed mostly of students for whom Spanish was their first language. The Spanish culture was the culture in which they were reared. College students are notorious for filling in all of the blanks on their exams, even when they do not have a clue as to the correct answer. Among students is a theory that if you leave a blank unfilled, it will be graded as incorrect. If you fill the blank with something, even though wrong, the teacher or grader may miss it and inadvertently grade the question correct. So, all blanks are filled with something. When the course is Bible and the culture is Hispanic, interesting answers are offered. I had asked on an exam, "The wilderness diet of John the Baptist consisted of _____ and _____." I hoped for a correct biblical answer of locust and wild honey. On one desperate student's exam, I read his answer of "locust and *frijoles.*" Since I've always encouraged creativity and given credit for creative answers, I gave the student full credit. However, had I been John the Baptist, I'd have kept the wild honey in my diet and substituted the refried beans for the locust.

Contradictory messages

The so-called "Jesus Revolution" took place while I was at Pan American University. During this time students used messages on just about everything to proclaim their faith. They used T-shirts, automobile bumper stickers, hats, textbook covers, and anywhere else you could think to share it. The Christian messages were so popular that often times they appeared in strange places. At a flea market, I saw a T-shirt that boldly proclaimed, "On Fire for Jesus." Unfortunately the wearer had a booth which was selling nude playing cards.

Commerce, TX

My second assignment in student ministry was East Texas State University situated in Commerce, TX (now Texas A&M University in Commerce). Moving to Commerce was a cultural experience in itself. The population of the student body was larger than was the population of the town. The student body was a mix of urbanites from nearby Dallas and rural folks from the dozens of small towns in the area. When we went to Commerce to look for a house, we had to stay in the lone motel which appeared as if it had been built around the turn of the century—the 20th century. I remember the clerk explaining to me that I could have a room with a tub or a room with a shower. I asked what was the difference. The clerk gave me a puzzled look and said, "with a tub, you sit down."

Students were notorious for putting their own signs next to the city-limits sign. One sign said, "Welcome to Commerce, the Eighth Wonder of the World." Then in smaller letters it explained the wonder as, "The only hole above ground." Holidays obviously left the town fairly empty as students, faculty, staff, and other employees took advantage of a chance to leave Commerce. On one such holiday I saw a sign at the city limits that read, "Last one out, please turn off the lights."

Favorite song . . . wrong place to admit it

I confess that I am a serious Willie Nelson fan. I even have a personalized autographed picture of him hanging in my office. I did not realize what impact my love of his country music had on my daughter. Danna was 2-years old when we moved to Commerce. Shortly after our arrival, I received a phone call one Sunday afternoon from Danna's Sunday-school teacher. She was horrified that the new campus minister in town had such an irreverent daughter. Seems the teacher had asked the little girls what their favorite songs were. She obviously expected, "Jesus Loves Me" or some other such Christian children's song. Danna yelled out, "Whiskey River Take My Mind" (by none other than Willie Nelson). All my attempted explanation did absolutely no good. Three years later we moved to Austin, where even Sunday-school teachers love Willie.

International diplomacy

One summer we decided to take a busload of international students to a professional baseball game. The Texas Rangers were playing in Arlington, less than 100 miles away. We knew we would have to explain much of the game to these international visitors since the game of baseball was as foreign to some of them as they were to us. The game was exciting and became heated toward the end when the umpire called a strike on one of the Ranger players who did not agree. An argument ensued between the Ranger and the umpire. Soon fans joined in the argument and called the umpire various names, some of which were not in the international students' English dictionary. Then one of the Americans in our group joined in the argument. Standing to his feet, he yelled loudly to the Ranger player, "Wrap the bat around his neck!" Another American quickly pulled the loud one back to his seat and reminded him of our now-astonished guests. On the bus ride back to Commerce the conversation in the back of the bus grew louder and louder. It was obvious that a heated discussion was under way. In the midst of it I heard an international student shout in broken English, "Wrrrrrap zie bot avound hees nek!" So much for ministry to international students.

Ag major from Frog Knot, TX

Some of the most unforgettable characters I've ever met were collegians. I met Hal Cunnyngham during his first day on campus as a freshman. I'll never forget asking him where he was from and hearing him proudly reply, "Ag major from Frog Knot, TX, Sir". As if I needed more information, he continued, "We've got a frog on the water tower." Thinking maybe I might misunderstand, Hal added, "Not a real one. He'd fall off and hurt himself." During Hal's sophomore year I invited him into my office to look over summer mission possibilities. An agriculture major was needed in Feni, Bangladesh. Long story short, Hal applied and was appointed. His first airplane ride was 14 hours. "The plane stopped in Honolulu, but I was afraid if I got off it, I'd never find the right plane again," Hal explained. Later he told me he only applied for summer missions because he thought Bangladesh was in Louisiana.

'Til what do us part?

One of the joys of working with university students is performing so many weddings. Whatever the generation, college students still get the urge to merge, so weddings are frequent occurrences. One wedding I will never forget is that of Cynthia Dement and you guessed it—Hal Cunnyngham. Before the wedding I had been having significant allergy problems so was on several prescription medications, including a very strong antihistamine that made my vision blur at times. I remember watching both brides come down the aisle amazed at how much they both looked like Cynthia. I think she was the two most beautiful brides I'd ever seen at the same wedding. I remember looking down toward my notes and trying to decide which Bible to read from since I appeared to be holding two of them. Because of the medication, I was sweating profusely from the candles, which were located too close behind me for comfort. I assumed my sweat was the cause for Hal and Cynthia to be so wide-eyed. Then I smelled something burning. The ivy behind me, also located too close to the candles, had caught fire. Thinking first the ivy then the preacher, I rushed through the remainder of the ceremony. Between the medicine, the candles, and the burning ivy, I'm not sure we got all of the vows repeated, but the Cunnynghams are still happily married, so I guess it worked.

Breathless in the invitation time

I was assisting with the decision time at a college student convention. The auditorium was one of those whose aisles sloped from back to front at a rather severe degree. Looking up the aisle during the third verse I saw her walking down the aisle. She was extremely large and was picking up momentum as she walked literally, "down the aisle." I calculated that she was not going to be able to slow down—much less stop—so I braced myself and placed one foot behind the other. As she approached, she opened her arms and hit me with a bear hug, lifting me completely off the floor, and setting me down at least a foot behind where I had originally stood. Not only did she move me, she knocked about half of the wind out of me. In my best gasping voice, I asked, "Yeeeessss?" I'm just glad she felt inclined to do all the talking from that point on. I have no memory of what her decision was, but I know what mine was—never work an invitation in an auditorium with aisles sloping downward when overweight people are in the crowd.

Clothes, half off

On my first day as Baptist student director at the University of Texas in Austin, I walked down Guadelupe Street, better known as "The Drag." This was August. The students were not wearing much in the way of clothing. So I was not surprised to see a large sign in the window of a clothing store, "Women's Clothes, Half Off." If that's the way they sell them, no wonder that's the way they wear them. Many students in those days dressed down. That is, they looked as sloppy as they could. One student told me he was down in the dumps when he bought his clothes. They not only looked it, they smelled like he had purchased them in the dumps.

Upper deck, Memorial Stadium

With great anticipation I attended my first football game in Memorial Stadium. I had long known of the mighty Texas Longhorns and the great traditions they held. To actually watch them play in their huge stadium was a dream-come-true for me. However, our tickets were on one of the top rows of the upper deck. I'm not sure how high the upper deck is, but a guy seated on the end of our row wore a white robe and held a harp. Of course, he could have just wandered into the stadium off Guadelupe Street. My seat must have been rather high, because my view of the game was continually being obstructed by the TV blimp passing in front.

Please don't pray for my wife

While I was serving as the Baptist campus minister at the University of Texas, one my faithful prayer partners was Ron Wells, who occupied the same position at Texas A&M University. One year we decided to have a joint staff retreat at a place half way between Austin and College Station. A time of relaxation and renewal, the retreat provided lots of opportunity for playing games and praying together. On the first night of the retreat, Vicki Spencer, wife of UT Bible instructor Rick Spencer, shared a tearful prayer request. She and Rick had tried unsuccessfully to get pregnant, so she wanted us to pray for them. In his God-sounding bass voice Ron said, "Let's pray right now!" We circled around Rick and Vicki. Ron laid hands on each of their shoulders and prayed a simple, direct prayer. "God, Vicki and Rick want to get pregnant. We want You to help them . . . tonight." Nine months from that night, Vicki and Rick welcomed their first-born child into the world. I remember when Rick told me that Vicki was pregnant, I immediately called Ron and told him, "Please, don't pray for my wife any more and don't be laying hands on her either."

The final results are In; they are better than expected.

During our years in Austin, our son James began his boyhood baseball career with t-ball. On one occasion James was playing in centerfield, which is where they put the next-to-the-least experienced player on the team. Right field was reserved for the least-experienced kid, since no one ever hit the ball to right field. Few hit it to center field, but on this day one kid did—a screeching line drive that bounced a couple of times before arriving at where James was bent over picking daisies. We were ahead by one run in the final inning. The other team had a runner on first base with two outs. The ball hit James in the glove. Standing up, James threw the ball toward the infield. This was scary since we never knew for sure where the ball was going when James threw it. This time he threw a perfect peg to the second baseman, who for some unknown reason was standing on second base. The ball hit the second baseman in the glove and stuck. A split-second later the runner from first base arrived. "Out!" yelled the umpire. We won! James was a new hero. Everyone was patting him where you pat heroes. Going home in the car, James asked me if he had made a good throw. As I was trying to tell him what a great throw it was, he interrupted with "Dad, I was throwing it to the pitcher." In t-ball, the kids are taught to throw the ball to the pitcher. As soon as the ball arrives inside the circle around the pitcher's mound, the other team's runners have to stop running. James aimed at the right place, but the results were better than he ever dared to dream.

Coaching nightmares

Several of my students from the University of Texas graduated and became coaches. Paul Gustafson shared the following account of his basketball coaching days:

"In 1981-83 I coached in Kemp, TX. All our games were someone's homecoming, which gives you an idea of how crummy we were—at all levels. In my first year I coached the 7th grade basketball team. We only won our first game against Crandall. The score was 6-4— in double overtime. Later that year we were playing the Grand Saline 7th graders. With about two minutes left in the game we were losing 76-24. One of my bench warmers, an astute tactician of the game, looked up at the scoreboard and made the brilliant observation, 'We gotta do something fast!'"

Another coach, David Brewer, told of having an offensive football lineman who was so dumb he could never remember who to block on each play called by the quarterback. One day, David had a brilliant idea. He called the lineman over then asked to see the palm of his hand. Drawing an arrow on the boy's hand, David, said, "Now when you line up, look at this hand; wherever the arrow points, you block that guy." David said this plan worked well until the day the dumb lineman looked at his hand upside down and blocked himself out of the play.

You might be a student minister If . . .

My good friend Richard Ross, professor of student ministry at Southwestern Baptist Seminary, allowed me to use the following list entitled "You might be a student minister if . . .."

• *You know over 50 things to do with a lighted candle on a student trip.*

• *You evaluate your student devotionals by how many cry.*

• *Your own children have never worn anything at night except student T-shirts.*

• *A sweet, little old lady tells you she is just sure that God is going to call you to the ministry some day.*

• *You suddenly discover you are sitting in a McDonald's without the student group—and you like the food.*

• *Your aunt still asks you what you are going to do when you grow up.*

• *You have washed every car in town but your own.*

• *You don't remember to gas the bus before leaving on a 1,000-mile student trip.*

• *You understand that going out to pick up the morning paper means gathering toilet paper.*

• *Your idea of worship leadership is a dynamic announcement time.*

• *You accidentally plan a lock-in the night of your wedding anniversary, but promise your spouse you will make it a special evening together anyway.*

• *You get a little thrill when you see a sign that says, "Bus drivers eat free."*

• *Your first question to an incoming freshman is, "Do you own a mini-van?"*

• *You have ever been inclined to violence when someone greets you returning from a student retreat with "how was your vacation?*

Chapter Six

On the Road Again

For three-and-a-half years I served as a national consultant with the Southern Baptist Home Mission Board (now the North American Mission Board). Someone defined a consultant as "anyone with a briefcase who is more than 100 miles from home." By that definition I was indeed a consultant. During my time with the board I averaged more than 15 days per month away from home. Willie Nelson sang my theme song, "On the Road Again." My long-time friend from college days, Daniel Sanchez, helped me understand what exactly a consultant was. Seems a guy was driving in the countryside when he encountered a sheepherder and his sheep. Stopping he asked, "If I can tell you how many sheep you have, can I have one?" "Sure," replied the sheep-herder. "159" said the traveler. "Amazing, take your pick," replied the sheep-herder. After a few minutes the sheep-herder spoke again. "If I can tell you what you do for a living, can I have my animal back?" "Fair enough," said the traveler. "You are a consultant." "How'd you know?" asked the traveler. Said the sheepherder, "You showed up unannounced and told me what I already knew. Now can I have my dog back?"

Chewing gum didn't help

I had never flown much before I moved to Atlanta, GA, but in the next 40 months I would achieve advanced frequent-flyer status with three airlines. Terminology was a bit of a problem in the early days. I spent a lot of time looking for a "gate" on the first trip to the Atlanta airport. I had no real fear of flying, although the fear of crashing was rather disturbing. I refused to think about the fact that many airports have the word "terminal" in their title. "Non-stop" flights were contrary to what I wanted—namely, to stop at the destination. I believed flight attendants could have used a phrase other than "final approach" to describe the pre-landing activity. I received several pieces of advice from colleagues. One said to sit in the rear of the plane, because you never hear of a plane backing into a mountain. Another offered the fact that gum would keep my ears from popping. He was correct, but it took several hours to get all of the gum out of my ears after I landed.

Rounding third and heading for the emergency room

The church where we were members in Georgia had a very active adult softball league. Pete Rose and I were the same age, and he was still playing. Why shouldn't I play? Of course for me, the gamble was taking the field. One night I was on first base when a teammate hit a long drive between the right and center fielder. As I headed for third base, the college-age third-base coach was waving me home. It wasn't his fault. He had no idea how old I was. For a few seconds, I forgot how old I was. My heart, which often writes checks that my body can't cash, said, "Go for it!" My mind said "You old fool, stop on third!" Suddenly while I was running full speed, I decided to stop. I heard a rather loud pop; I was on the ground in great pain. Up to that moment in time I had never heard of a hamstring. A few days later I retired from softball and bought some new golf equipment.

A misprint got it right

One of the wonderful privileges of working for the Home (North American) Mission Board was sharing each spring what

God was doing in North America through the Annie Armstrong Easter Offering. My first Easter of employment found me assigned to several churches for the purpose of giving a report. As always, we had a theme and brochures printed for mass distribution. This particular year the theme was, *"By love serve one another,"* a quote from Galatians 5:13. As I sat on the front row of my first church, I was waiting my turn on the program and looking over the brochure. On the inside cover I glanced at the Scripture reference. Then I looked again. Could it be? The brochure read, Galatians 5:15, not Galatians 5:13. I quickly opened my Bible to double-check the reference. While the theme was actually based on verse 13, the brochure was printed incorrectly and referenced the theme as being in verse 15. These were the early days of the Southern Baptist Convention controversy (or Conservative Resurgence as it would later be called). Many people were accusing others of various beliefs and practices. As I read verse 15, I thought how a mistake in the print shop was so prophetic. Verse 15 reads, *"If you bite and devour one another, beware lest you be consumed by one another."* It was humorous but not very funny.

Surprise, surprise, surprise!

Not to be outdone the Baptist Bulletin Service printed thousands of bulletin inserts with the seven surprises for the Christian who begins to tithe. It was an impressive list complete with the biblical admonition to give as recorded in 2 Corinthians 9:7. The biggest surprise must have occurred when the printer discovered too late that the title of the insert—"7 Suprises" — misspelled the word Surprise.

Surrounded by witnesses?

The annual Home Mission Board retreat always produced a few good laughs. One year we had a well-known motivational speaker who was less familiar with his audience than with his subject. In a room full of ordained, if not orderly, Baptist ministers the misguided speaker began to use an illustration from the horse-racing business. "Suppose you were at the races and had bet all your money on one long-shot horse," he said, as we tried to act knowledgeable. The speaker continued, "As the horses round the final turn and head down the home stretch, your horse moves into the lead. Approaching the finish line, your horse increases the lead. Now tell me, what are you doing at this time?" A long silence followed as we tried to decide whether we should give an informed answer or intentionally give a wrong answer and thus continue job security. Finally the silence was broken by my friend Herman Rios, who said, "I'm looking around to see if anyone there knows me."

Low on brain power

An informational meeting regarding new insurance coverage had raised many questions. Everyone but the few question-askers had grown weary of the discussion. A certain back-row employee, known for his attempts to keep everything on the lighter side, said to the representative, "My friend here needs brain-transplant surgery, but I don't see it on the list of surgeries covered by this new insurance." The classic reply was, "Sir, if you are the donor, it would be listed under Minor Surgery."

One Bible fits all

Our children were still young when I was traveling so much. However the times when I was at home and attended church with them were mostly memorable. We were never sure how much age difference between two kids would have been perfect, but we were sure it was not two-and-a-half years. One of many disagreements happened on a Sunday as we were leaving church where we had heard how much we ought to love one another. In the course of the argument Danna said, "*My* Bible says . . ." with strong emphasis on the word "*My.*" James, a child of few words, replied concerning Bibles and Danna's "*My*" emphasis, "Don't they all?"

Bulletin Bloopers

Thousands, maybe millions, of church-bulletin bloopers exist—misprints that speak volumes of subtle truth. Traveling the country and being in many different churches I was allowed the privilege of enjoying many of these bloopers. These I have actually seen with my own eyes. In the section explaining how to join a particular church, the sentence read, "Acknowledge that you have sinned and ask God to forgive your *sings.*" In another church where the popular *Experiencing God* program was being studied on Sunday evenings the bulletin proclaimed, "No Experiencing God tonight." In still another church I had sent my sermon title in advance for the bulletin. I was preaching on the "Hours of Joy" from Hebrews 12:2 where it says Jesus, "*for the joy that was set before Him endured the cross,*" (for six hours). Much to my surprise the special musical solo preceding my sermon was printed in the bulletin—"*How Tedious and Tasteless the Hours.*" While I did not actually see all of these, I was told about them by those who supposedly saw them. But you know how these things make the rounds.

6:30 p.m., Monday night: Couples covered-dish dinner. Followed by prayer and medication.

The music ministry of the church invites all who enjoy sinning to be present Wednesday evening at 7:45 p.m. for rehearsal.

Please remember in prayer those who are sick of our church.

No healing service Sunday night due to the pastor's illness. The Fasting & Prayer Conference includes meals.

The Choir will sing Christmas carols Monday night at the Old Folks Rest Room.

Ladies, don't forget the church rummage sale. It's a chance to get rid of those things not worth keeping. Bring your husbands.

Next Sunday morning our beloved pastor will preach his farewell sermon following by a choir special, "Break Forth with Joy."

The new youth minister will speak briefly at the service tonight. Let us rejoice.

Hymn # 204 "O Rest in the Lard"

The peacemaking meeting scheduled for today has been canceled due to a conflict.

The church will host an evening of fine dining, super entertainment, and gracious hostility.

Low-Self-Esteem Support Group will meet Thursday at 7:00 p.m. Please use the back door.

Weight Watchers will meet Friday at 7:00 p.m. Please use the large double doors at the side entrance.

The evening sermon title is "What Hell is Like." Come early and hear the choir rehearse.

The bulletin listed the sermon title as "Hell" and the hymn following as "Tell Mother I'll be There in Answer to Her Prayer."

Morning sermon: "Jesus Walks on the Water." Evening sermon: "Searching for Jesus."

Job descriptions

Shortly after my arrival as an employee at the Home Mission Board, someone sent this inner-office memo defining the following job descriptions for the board personnel. Since I have seen several versions of this document, I am not real sure it was originated for the Home Mission Board, although some of the descriptions were very accurate.

President—
Able to leap tall buildings in a single bound;
Is more powerful than a locomotive;
  Is faster than a speeding bullet;
  Walks on water;
  Talks with God.
Vice President— Is able to leap short buildings in a single
  bound.
  Is as powerful as a switch engine;
  Is just as fast as a speeding bullet;
  Walks on water if the sea is calm;
  Talks with God.
Division Director— Leaps short buildings with a running
  start.
  Is almost as powerful as a switch engine;
  Is faster than a speeding BB;
  Walks on water if he knows where stumps are;
  Talks with God if special request is approved.
Department Director— Clears a Quonset hut.
  Loses race with a locomotive;
  Can fire a speeding bullet;
  Swims well;
  Is occasionally addressed by God.
Consultant— Runs into small buildings.
  Recognizes locomotive two out of three times;
  Used a squirt gun while in college;
  Knows how to use the water fountain;
  Mumbles to himself.
Secretary— Lifts buildings to walk under them.
  Kicks locomotives off the track;
  Catches speeding bullets in her teeth;
  Freezes water with a single glance;
  When God speaks, she says, "May I ask who is calling?"

I included these job descriptions for your benefit. I fail to see much humor in them. I was a consultant.

Killing Rumors

One of the jobs of a consultant was to kill rumors that tend to become fact if not corrected. Ten of the more widespread rumors we faced in dealing with Baptists around the country were:

1. *John the Baptist founded the Southern Baptist Convention.*
2. *One should never sit on the front row or sing the third verse.*
3. *God's presence is best felt on the back row of the auditorium.*
4. *The first persons to arrive in the worship center should sit on the end of the row.*
5. *A sermon is measured by the amount of sweat produced by the preacher.*
6. *Fellowship is from the Greek word meaning food.*
7. *Jesus actually turned water into Welch's grape juice.*
8. *When the roll is called up yonder, you'll be expected to bring a covered dish.*
9. *The mission statement of the church is "We've never done it that way before."*
10. *King James was the brother of Jesus, both of whom spoke King James English.*

What kind of what am I?

During our time in Atlanta our daughter grew into her teen-age years. Before she became totally teen-age rebellious—and while she was still somewhat child-like naïve—she offered us a much-remembered moment. Having grown up mostly in Texas where barbecue meant beef, she was unfamiliar with signs in southeastern pork barbecue restaurants. As was her custom, she excused herself shortly after the family entered a barbecue restaurant. On entering a restaurant Danna always needed to make a trip to the restroom . This time, she returned faster than usual with a perplexed look on her face. "Dad" she whispered. "Am I a Boar or a Sow?"

Catfish buffet . . . priceless!

Speaking of food, my wife and I found one of those southern, all-you-dare-to-eat buffets that advertised a Friday night special of whole fried catfish. We do love fried catfish—especially on Friday night. We timed our arrival perfectly as the first wave of diners were leaving, and thus clearing out some space for us. As they departed, they were discussing the need to hurry, lest they be late for Friday Night Wrestling at the Dixie Hall Ballroom. Together we put away six whole catfish. I'll let someone else do the long division to figure who ate how much. We pretty much had free reign of the potatoes, cabbage, red beans and rice, corn-on-the-cob, etc. Of course no one was bothering the salad bar. They might as well not have had a soup bar. All was going well until I encountered significant difficulty at the dessert bar. A rather large woman was standing with her arms crossed, blocking about one-third of the area. As I approached, she smiled, revealing an absolute dental nightmare. I immediately felt guilty for having so many teeth. Then she spoke. "They comin' with more cheesecake." With a sudden dislike for cheesecake, I moved on down the line to the lemon pie. Seeing I had my dessert, Bubba John, our 300-pound waiter, asked, "You 'ant your coffee now?" I was afraid to decline. Needless to say, I left a large tip. Whole fried catfish and an evening of entertainment—priceless!

Back To reality

The revival services in the West Virginia church were going extremely well. Numerous decisions had been recorded in each service. Attendance was growing. The people were very loving: they hugged me and told me how much they appreciated me. My ego was being stroked. I was having a great week. During the fourth service of the revival meeting the pastor called on one of the leaders of the church to begin the service in prayer. This man had just eaten dinner with me the night before and had gone out of his way to be friendly to me—even making some connections to people we both knew in the past. I felt good about his affirmation of me and his encouragement each night of the revival meeting. I really liked the guy. To my amazement, he prayed, "And Lord, help our pastor and this other guy who has been with us this week." Just when you think you are something special, God sends someone to bring you back to reality. I've had a steady stream of them.

Students or senior adults?

A friend I met in my travels sent me a note about one who switched to the position of senior-adult minister from a long tenure as a youth/student minister. Seems he had listed five reasons why the new senior-adult minister was enjoying his new group more than he enjoyed working with youth:

- *With senior adults you don't get phone calls after 10 p.m.*
- *With senior adults you never have to deal with angry parents.*
- *With senior adults you can use the same material over and over because most don't remember it.*
- *With senior adults you never have to counsel with an unwanted pregnancy.*
- *With senior adults, they're supposed to be on drugs.*

Chapter Seven

Back on the Hill

The next chronological chapter of my life took place at Southwestern Baptist Theological Seminary in Fort Worth, TX, humbly referred to by "Southwesterners" as "the largest theological school in the world". Whether it was actually the largest was a question that was never raised. Being a professor of evangelism and missions, I certainly did not see it as a part of my job description to raise the question.

Illogical logic

Besides being called "the largest theological school in the world", Southwestern was also situated on the highest point of elevation in Tarrant County, thus earning it the logical title of "Seminary Hill." This became the subject of many jokes throughout the years especially from students who arrived from areas of the country such as Colorado and North Carolina, where majestic mountains dot the landscape. These jokes were never understood by students who arrived from flatlands such as Kansas and west Texas. I'm not sure if this logical title had anything to do with the missing letters on the highway sign. One day someone — likely students from Arkansas — removed the letter "o" from the seminary sign on Interstate 35, causing the sign to read: "Southwestern The logical Seminary."

Calling the hogs on Seminary Hill

Speaking of folks from Arkansas, an event happened shortly after the seminary installed video monitors in all classrooms so professors who ran out of lecture notes could show video-tapes. Located in the basement of Scarborough Hall is a bust of Charles Haddon Spurgeon, the famous British Baptist preacher and provider of many a sermon for struggling student-pastors. Occasionally the classroom monitors would be on during the first class of a particular day sharing an announcement or prayer request. So it was not unusual to arrive in the classroom on a particular morning and find the video monitor on. Expecting some announcement on the screen, most professors left the monitors on. Unknown was the fact that certain professors of the Arkansas lineage had made a video tape and submitted it to the media office with the request that it be shown at the beginning of the next day. Thus the first scene on the monitor this particular day was the bust of Spurgeon. As the camera panned back to expose a larger view, it became obvious Spurgeon was wearing a Hog Hat. If you don't know what a Hog Hat is, consider yourself among the blessed. A Hog Hat is a red plastic hat in the shape of a hog, complete with snout. People of the Razorback persuasion normally (or is it abnormally?) wear these hats at all University of Arkansas football games and any other occasion that suits the sub-culture. This day found Spurgeon wearing a Hog Hat. Before most slow-of-foot professors could turn off the video monitors, sounds were heard from off-screen. Various professors, whose family trees were planted in the Arkansas hills, were heard "calling the hogs." Again, if you have never heard this "call", you are of all most blessed. It is a high pitched, "Soooeeeeee! Pig!" call making Razorback blood run hot and others run cold. Personally, I haven't preached a Spurgeon sermon since.

Two legends face off

Fierce competition was not limited to Arkansas football fans. One day in the faculty lounge (which with all due respect should have been called "The Faculty Room") two well-known professors got into a rather heated discussion as to which one of them was the best football lineman in high school. One was an offensive guard, the other a defensive tackle. After some time a third faculty member tired of the debate and challenged the two to get out of their chairs and show us who was the best. Now we had two 60-something-year-olds, distinguished academicians, dressed in suits and ties assuming a three-point stance a yard apart. Someone at the table said, "Hut! Hut Hut!" and they went at each other. For a good two to three minutes they grunted, struggled, panted, and pushed until finally as if they had heard a higher voice, they both fell on their backs on the carpet and continued their heavy breathing for a few more minutes. Nothing was settled in regard to football, but New Testament survey and missiology will never seem the same to me again.

A "friend" helps with hernia surgery

I returned to Fort Worth from a sabbatical leave in Germany with a hernia from carrying my wife's luggage. The day before I went to the hospital for this surgery, a "friend" sent me a list of things I did not want to hear the doctor say during surgery. It wasn't very funny at the time, but looking back it has gained a degree of humor.

Better save that, we may need it for the autopsy.
Someone call the custodian, we'll need a mop.
Accept this sacrifice, O Great Lord of Darkness.
Spot, come back with that. Bad dog!
Wait a minute, if this is the hernia, what is that?
Hand me that, uh . . . that uh . . . thingie.
Oooooooo, did you ever see that much blood come out of one of those?
Ooops, page 48 of the manual is missing.
Sterile, schmeril, the floor's clean, right?

Everyone stand back, I lost my contact lens.
What do you mean he wasn't in for a sex change?

Preaching professors and student-preachers

One day my faculty colleague, preaching professor Jimmie Nelson, told me the following story of his first days on the seminary faculty:

"After over 20 years of being a pastor I became a professor at Southwestern Baptist Seminary. I was given several keys including one for my office and one for the faculty lounge. Early one morning thinking I was the only person there, I decided to admit myself to the faculty lounge. I had always held faculty members in high esteem and could not believe I was now one of them. I looked both ways down the hall as I inserted the key, feeling I was intruding. Inside sat professor of preaching Dr. H.C. Brown, sitting at the table looking through his morning mail. I said, 'Hello, Dr. Brown'. He replied, 'Huh, uh, Jimmie, it's H.C. For the first three months you will be wondering how you got here. After that you'll wonder why any of us ever got here'. That was a great icebreaker welcome for me."

Jimmie also shared the story of a student-preacher:

"Preaching lab was always a fun place to be. One day a middle-aged student, a military veteran, was to preach. His text for the sermon was read from the epistle to the Philippians. He then began his sermon by saying that we probably did not know much about these people to whom Paul wrote but that he had worked with these 'Filipinos' when stationed there during the war. And he referred to these 'Filipinos' several times in the course of the sermon! The response was hilarious and gracious."

Vacationing in my 60th summer

In the early days of my 60th summer, having completed 16 years on the seminary faculty, I reasoned that we ought to take a real vacation—go somewhere with nothing to do when we arrived. Since my earliest vacations, I had learned from my preacher-father that vacation is something you do on the way to the Southern Baptist Convention. Don't get me wrong. While my friends were spending a summer week at Grandma's, I was exploring exotic sites along America's highways between Texas and wherever the convention met that summer—Atlantic City, Chicago, San Francisco, Los Angeles, New Orleans, St. Louis, and so forth. My September school reports on "How I Spent My Summer" were always exciting, even if the teacher occasionally didn't believe me.

Thus when I became a man, I did not put away childish things. Our family vacations were always taken on the way to some conference I was leading or attending. When my kids were asked in school to define the word *vacation* they would most likely respond with, "Glorieta." Most summers found my family "vacationing" in the beautiful Sangre de Cristo Mountains of New Mexico while I led a conference during College Student Week at Glorieta Baptist Conference Center.

So since I was nearing 60, I decided the time had arrived for a vacation where I had no responsibility, no assignment, and nothing to do. When would we go in a summer already crowded with speaking engagements? Ah, here was a week in August—the seminary's fall semester was still a few weeks away. Perfect. Where would we go to do this nothing business? Somewhere with no TV, no Internet, no phone calls, no schedule. One e-mail confirmed a friend's cabin was indeed available at—you guessed it—Glorieta Conference Center in New Mexico. (By the way, at some point in time, the word "Baptist" was removed from the title so the rest of the world could enjoy Glorieta . . . and help Baptists pay for it!) Little did we know that the week we so carefully selected was "Collegiate Week" at Glorieta. It had been 15 years since we had attended Collegiate Week (known in earlier years as Student Week). Holy Late-Night Programming!

We arrived at Glorieta late on Sunday night after several hours of driving across beautiful West Texas, where you can take a nap as someone else drives and wake up wondering if you've been anywhere. The first night we had less than four hours sleep. Amazing what an altitude of 7,200 feet does to the sleep patterns of flatland 60-year-olds. We awakened with pounding headaches. We had not yet been to a worship service.

Monday's main agenda called for some of that great New Mexican food in nearby Santa Fe. Wonder if that same place was still open on Cerrillos Road? It was. We ate big. A faster-than-usual drive back to Glorieta was prompted by the green chili on top of the spicy pork enchiladas. Funny, but green chili never seemed to be that hot before! This called for a nap, from which I awakened with the same headache, plus a stuffy nose. So now that we've adjusted to the altitude, let's go to the evening worship service. We arrived five minutes late. The auditorium was dark. A spotlight was on the band; someone had turned the volume to "excessively loud." In the roar of the music I'm not sure what my wife said, but I understood one adjective as I followed her out of the door. We went back to the quietness of the cabin, ate some ice cream, and went to bed early.

Tuesday dawned with me having the same altitude headache. I thought I remembered these headaches going away after one day. Maybe it was lingering because of the stomach problems I was having from the green chili. I had planned to play golf this day, but everyone was talking about a "new restaurant" near Glorieta. Not to age so gracefully, we headed for the "new restaurant." In that day "new restaurants" near Glorieta seemed to pop up annually. Funny, but the people running it always looked like the ones who ran last year's "new restaurant." This year's "new restaurant" served great turkey enchiladas. However they appeared to be covered with last year's green chili. You talk about hot! It was hotter than a five-alarm fire on the outskirts of hell. More stomach problems. Another nap. Was that thunder I heard while I slept or my 60-year old stomach rebelling? And why did I awake feeling more tired than when I went to sleep? Maybe some more ice cream would help. It didn't. We skipped the evening worship service and went to bed early.

Wednesday we left Glorieta, headache intact, and all attempts to re-live the past. We moved on up the road looking for a Luby's Cafeteria. Maybe we'll return to Glorieta next year, maybe not. I wonder if Glorieta still has those Chautauqua conferences for senior adults?

Take cover

I was to represent the seminary at a rural associational meeting of churches. I arrived early enough to hear the pre-service workshop on how to get churches ready for Y2K. The speaker, well-trained in shock techniques, had the mostly older crowd worried sick about the horrible effects of the millennium change. Then he introduced his new book on how to avoid these effects. Following his presentation, a retired pastor got up to close the workshop time in prayer and preceded the prayer with his own version of Y2K prevention. "Back when I was in another church, the radio *comed* on and said 'Warnin', tornado alert! Take cover.' So I went to the bedroom, got in bed and pulled up the cover. After a short nap the tornado threat was gone. So on December 31, I'm gonna take cover." So much for high-tech prevention.

Passing the plate

Recently I was running uncomfortably close to the time for a revival service to begin. I had driven back to Fort Worth the night before to teach my Tuesday classes. I was to return afterward to the Oklahoma town where the revival services were being held. I had been reviewing my notes and was ready to

80

preach. I just needed to get there. That's when I came up behind the slowest driver in eastern Oklahoma. Late-model station wagon . . . wife in front seat . . . no apparent concerns. The road was narrow. The yellow stripe was double. No passing. So I got on his back bumper. I flashed my lights. I honked my horn. I called him several senior-adult names. No response. If anything, he seemed to slow down even more. After several miles of frustration I saw my opening. I rushed around him being sure to cut back quickly so as to make my point. Now it was open road to the church. I left him in the dust.

I actually arrived with a few minutes to spare, minutes that were spent shaking hands with people near the back door of the church—the door toward which the slow driver and his wife soon approached. Seeing them, I headed away from the door toward the pastor, who was already at the front of the auditorium.

"Do you recognize the couple that just entered?" I asked him.

"Sure," he replied "He's one of our senior deacons. Why, do you know him?"

"Oh, no," I responded. "He just looks familiar."

"Yeah," continued the pastor, "he's the biggest giver in the church."

A few nights later, when I looked at my love offering check, I wondered how much that bumper-pushing, horn-honking, fast-passing experience cost me. You could say I gave new meaning to "passing the plate."

Fastest answer to prayer

Mrs. Lucille Glasscock, a former seminary student, gave a considerable amount of money to construct the seminary's World Missions and Evangelism Center, which was understandably named after her. She was invited to travel from Corpus Christi, TX, to Fort Worth to give the dedicatory prayer for the center. Because of her advanced years and ill health, the dedication was postponed several times. Finally she arrived and was accompanied by her personal nurse. In her prayer she said, "And God you know I never got the plaque that the seminary promised me . . .." I heard shuffling in the crowd and a door open, followed in a flash by a door opening again and more shuffling. After Mrs. Glasscock said "Amen", Dr. Russell Dilday, then-president of the seminary, handed the plaque to Mrs. Glasscock with the words, "Mrs. Glasscock, this may be the fastest answer to any prayer you ever prayed."

Bragging rights and bragging wrongs

A group of faculty colleagues, of which I was a part, used to eat lunch together every Friday. The rule was that if anyone mentioned the seminary, they had to buy everyone else's meal. In other words this was an end-of-the-work-week-forget-it-all meal. One of our group took great glee one week in bragging about a convenience-store clerk that had flirted with him as he made his purchase. Since we were all passed the age of being flirted with by anyone, this called for a group response. The next Friday a Fort Worth police officer (good friends with one of the group members) showed up at the restaurant and asked whether anyone knew who was driving the red pick-up in the parking lot. The truck, of course, belonged to our bragging group member. Then a warrant for arrest was read to our bewildered friend. The charge was sexual harassment. The warrant cited "an anonymous convenience store clerk". It included a number of "where-as" statements, the last of which was "Whereas you don't know when to brag and when not to brag in front of your poorly chosen friends . . .." The moral of this story is, if someone flirts with you, don't brag about it at lunch on Friday to a bunch of seminary professors who have been spiritual all week.

Chapter Eight

Interim Interludes

One of the genuine joys of serving on a seminary faculty is the privilege of also serving as interim pastor at many churches as well as speaking in many others. Each church provided its own humorous moments, some of which I had best not relay in this book.

Forced appreciation

One children's worker, no doubt in an attempt to get the children to exhibit more appreciation to members of their families, handed to each child paper plates and crayons. She asked them to write a note to a family member. She showed me one paper plate that read, "Thank you for being weird. I appreciate you because I have to." I was just glad she didn't ask them to write a note to the interim pastor.

An ego trip to the nursing home

Because the church where I was serving was on local-access television, I often was watched at a nearby nursing home. One Sunday a church member expressed to me how much her aging mother loved to hear me preach. She said her mother repeated my sermons almost verbatim to anyone in the nursing home who would listen. She further assured me how very much her mother would love to meet me. After several Sundays of this, I agreed to pay a visit to this faithful supporter of mine. I'll never forget meeting her and explaining to her who I was. I felt confident that she would just burst out in joyful tears at my presence.

After all, the interim pastor had taken time out of his crowded Sunday activities to pay a visit to the nursing home. You can imagine what an ego-blow I suffered when the dear old saint looked at me for several long seconds and said. "Now, who are you, Sonny?"

Older kids say the darndest things

I love senior adults. Sometimes, however, they can say the funniest things without meaning to do so. I was into my late 50s when a dear blue-haired lady came to me after my first sermon at a pastorless church. She asked, "I hear them say you was at the seminary?" "Yes, Ma'am." I proudly replied in my most distinguished faculty-sounding voice. "Hum!" She mused. "How long before you graduate?"

One night I preached on trust. I made some comments about how children have such a difficult time trusting when in their early years we teach them about the reality of the Easter Bunny and the Tooth Fairy. Then they get older and realize we deceived them. Immediately after the last "amen" of the service, an elderly woman was in my face. "You almost blew it!" she cried. "My grandson was here tonight and you almost blew Santa Claus' cover."

"Buried With Christ in Baptism, Raised to Laugh in Newness of Life"

Some of the funniest things that ever happen to preachers happen in the baptistery. In one interim pastorate I followed a pastor who was more than six-feet tall. When the first baptismal service occurred, the baptism committee filled the baptistery as usual and never observed my 5-foot-10-inch height. When I stepped into the baptistery, my waders started taking on water before anyone else entered the waters. If I had baptized many more people that night, I would not have been able to move out of the baptistery for being so waterlogged. After the sermon that night, a wet spot appeared behind the pulpit where I had dripped dry.

Another church had not baptized in many months. When the baptistery was filled, the water ran through rusty pipes. The lone candidate for baptism that night was a young, blond-haired boy. As I passed by him staring into the orange water, I assured him, "after you get baptized, you're hair will be that color." When he came up out of the water, unaware that I had a microphone on my tie, he asked for all to hear, "Is my hair orange now?"

Still another church moved into the new worship center while I was its interim pastor. Consequently I had the privilege of being the first one in the new baptistery—the new leaking baptistery. Apparently the fact that the tank wouldn't hold water was not known until I entered it. Because of the move to the new worship center, the church had a backlog of people awaiting baptism. The longer I baptized, the lower the water level descended. Practically lying on the floor of the baptistery, the last candidate truly was a low-water baptism. One more candidate and I'd been sprinkling instead of immersing.

Too many grandmothers

At the conclusion of a wedding ceremony the ushers failed to return to the front of the church to escort the grandmothers to the foyer. I could see the wedding party partying in the foyer but had no way to signal to them concerning the oversight. Meanwhile the organist continued to play the postlude. Finally someone in the foyer realized the problem. He or she sent the ushers rushing down the aisle for the fastest walking that most of these grandmothers had done in years. Still the organist completed the postlude before the last grandmother was removed from her pew and taken safely to the foyer. Finally, in silence, I was able to dismiss the audience to the reception. Walking by the organ and forgetting that my lapel microphone was still on, I exclaimed to the organist for all present to hear, "Had more grandmothers than we had music tonight, didn't we?" Needless to say the reception was rather tense where I stood.

No, no! deposit your offering in the offering plate!

In another interim pastorate, we were meeting in the family life center while waiting on the new auditorium to be completed. The family life center, which smelled a lot like a gymnasium, did not have the most airtight roof, because a bird somehow got into the service. For approximately 10 minutes in the midst of my sermon the bird soared and dove around the congregation. As ushers rushed quickly and quietly to open the doors in hopes of luring the wayward bird out of the building, the bird made a low swoop and dropped his Sunday morning offering on the head of an elderly lady. While most worshipers did not see this deposit, I did. That made it extremely difficult to keep on preaching with any degree of pastoral composure. All the while I was hoping the lady would deem my sermon worth the blessing she received.

Preaching was for the birds

I seem to have a problem preaching where birds are present. In another church where I was serving as interim pastor, we decided to move the Sunday night services in May to a nearby park. That seemed like such a great idea—bring the family, bring a picnic basket, bring your Bible, bring your friends, and so forth. The park had a sunken amphitheater in which we would have our worship service. One of those nights while I was preaching, a group of ducks appeared on the horizon. Seeing (or smelling) the leftover food in the baskets under the seats, they made a sharp nose-dive into the amphitheater. Then the ducks aimed at me; they flew only a few inches over my head as they departed the service. Having completely lost the attention of my now laughter-ridden audience—not to mention other losses—I had nothing to do but pray and dismiss.

Baby Sarah was not dead

We had prayed for many Sundays for little baby Sarah, who was quite ill. Sunday after Sunday, in this particular interim pastorate, I had reminded the folks to continue to pray for baby Sarah. One Sunday morning, as I was walking from the church office to the worship center, a lady handed me a note that read, "Baby Sarah died last night." At the conclusion of the worship service, during the announcements, I shared the solemn news that baby Sarah had died. Immediately after the service, a frantic church member came running up to me saying baby Sarah's grandmother had been listening to our service on the radio and had just called to say that baby Sarah was not dead but was improving rapidly and expected to live. Moral of the story: validate all announcements before making them.

A leak in my waders

I fell and broke my right shoulder, dislocated it, tore the rotator cuff, and did nerve damage. The fall was followed by a long rehabilitation period, during which I did not baptize anyone. Once the strength returned to my right shoulder, I resumed baptizing. This occurred in August just after summer youth camp. We had a large number of teen-agers to baptize. As I was waiting to enter the water, a question crossed my mind. I wondered whether rubber waders stored in a closet for many months could have cracked. One step into the water and I had my answer. As teen-ager after teen-ager came through the baptismal waters my waders slowly filled with water. "How long, O Lord, how long?" Fortunately the last teen-ager was baptized just before my waders completely water-logged. One more teenager and I would have preached the sermon from the baptistery.

I hoped it was my soft drink

My plan that Friday evening was to drive to the town in which I was serving as interim pastor of the First Baptist Church. My purpose was to watch the high-school football game. Understand that this was part of my ministry to the teenagers. Since the stadium hamburgers were about the best in town, I planned to have supper at the game. The closer I got to the town, the more brightly lightning lit up the sky. By the time I arrived, I had decided the kickoff would be delayed because of the storm, so I pulled into a convenience store and purchased some cheese crackers and a soft drink to hold me until game time.

Not wanting to sit in my car in the stadium parking lot, I headed to the church to wait out the storm. While on my cell phone with the minister of music, I saw lightning hit something ahead of me. I exclaimed, "Wow! I think lightening just hit the Church of Christ!" Unknown to me, his telephone went out after the word "Church". Thinking our church had been struck, the music minister made a mad dash to assess the damage. In the next few minutes, thinking I was still talking on the phone to a live human, I described what I later discovered was a tornado with winds in excess of 100-miles-per-hour. I drove by the First Baptist Church sign as it exploded with only my name as interim pastor left. Some of the elderly ladies who had been trying to talk me into being their permanent pastor said it was an omen. I assured them it was just good paint.

Proceeding to the church I drove over downed power lines, dodged spinning vehicles and falling trees, and was hit by flying debris causing many scrapes, scratches, and dents in my car. In the midst of this I was driving frantically toward the church and talking on my cell phone to an absent musician. Just as I got to the church, a pickup truck arrived looking for safety as well. When the wind stopped blowing, we both got out of our vehicles to see the church's steeple lying in the parking lot and observe the emergency vehicles that were looking for damage and injuries.

In the midst of the excitement, my new pickup-driving, snuff-dipping, Bud-Lite-hat-wearing, friend observed, "Hey!, yore pants is wet, and so's your car seat!" Realizing that even with his lack of education, he had made an accurate assessment, I nonchalantly replied, "Must have spilled my cola." At least I was hoping it was the soft drink.

Can I buy you a cup of coffee?

Sunday had been preceded by $1,250.00 worth of mechanical work on my Chevy that then was worth $4,000.00. About three miles from home on the way to my interim pastorate the "service-engine-soon" light came on. Obviously, the $1,250.00 didn't cover getting that light to stay off. I returned home, swapped vehicles, transferred all my stuff, and left again in my wife's mini-van. I placed my Bible in the driver's door compartment. Besides being frustrated by the dash light, I now was running later than I wanted to on my way to the church. But I needed coffee. Stopping at a convenience store, I quickly got my coffee and started to get back in the van. That's when the coffee cup turned upside down into the door compartment where my Bible was perched with its pages exposed upward. I didn't just spill coffee on my Bible; I poured a medium-size Styrofoam™ cup of coffee into the pages of my Bible. Not only did the coffee—with cream and sugar—saturate my Bible, but my sermon notes were virtually destroyed. I was too late to return home. I was already running a close-call for church. Standing in the pulpit for the call to worship, I held up my Bible and sermon notes and exclaimed to the congregation, "I know you can't see this very well from where you sit, but don't feel alone. I can't see it very well either." Explaining the morning chaos, I continued, "Since

I have no notes that I can read, this morning's sermon will likely be shorter than usual, depending on how much I remember." Sure enough the sermon was much too brief. Every time I looked down to my notes, I saw only coffee-stains. The morning wasn't a total loss, however. The next Sunday three deacons offered to buy me coffee.

Fleas on the preacher

The sanctuary was old, sacred, revered and in need of many things not the least of which was the work of a good exterminator. In between the two morning worship services the minister of music shared with me that fleas were now in the sanctuary. He wasn't sure if it was because of the rats under the floor, the rainy season, or just the age of the building. The previous Saturday he and his son had been in the sanctuary preparing for Sunday services. The son was barefooted. As they began to leave, the young son complained of something biting him on the feet. That's when the minister of music saw dozens of fleas on the child's feet and legs. Then he began to feel them on his body. On further examination he confirmed fleas on himself as well. At that point of his story, I began to itch myself. As soon as he had left the pastor's office, I headed for the men's room and my own ministerial flea examination. None were found, but I continued to sense their presence on my body throughout the 11 a.m. service. Perhaps because this bit of enlightening information was told to me by the minister of music, this caused me to remember an old, old country gospel song titled, "There Ain't No Flies on My Jesus." Then I thought of an appropriate second line—"But there's fleas on my preacher."

Unintentional interim

A former student invited me to preach in his church on the first Sunday after he left to take another pastorate. Just before I went to the pulpit to preach, the chairman of the deacons asked me to turn the service back over to him when I was finished rather than dismiss the congregation. Much to my surprise, when the deacon chairman took the pulpit, he announced the steps for a vote on "calling Dr. Crawford as interim pastor." No one had even mentioned that possibility to me, nor was I prepared to accept if they extended a call to me. Apparently my former student had told them to call me as interim. What I also did not know was that my former student had not left the church on the best of terms, so they were in no mood to listen to his advice. I let the vote take place (as if I could have stopped it) and then followed the men down the hall where they were to count the ballots. I stopped briefly in the restroom to let them have a few minutes before I told them this was a mistake. When I entered the church office, I told them I thought there had been a mistake. "Don't matter" said one of the ballot counters. "You didn't get enough votes anyway." In a day when the more popular term, "intentional interim" was being used, I was almost an unintentional interim.

Musical sermon

At one interim pastorate I had received an early Christmas gift—a beautiful tie that played "Jingle Bells" when the front of the tie was pushed. I wore it the following Sunday morning. Unfortunately in the midst of my sermon I leaned into the rather tall pulpit and set off the music. With the lapel mike located just an inch or so above the music box, all present including the TV audience heard the entire verse of "Jingle Bells." After the service one gracious member commented, "Best sermon I ever heard with music accompaniment." Another not-so-gracious member quipped, "Best sermon I ever heard from a ding-a-ling." It reminded me of a friend telling of a minister of music who visited a new widow to see what song she wanted sung at her husband's funeral. "His favorite song was 'Jingle Bells'," said the widow. Somewhat unsure the musician asked the pastor who replied, "If that's what she wants, sing it." Following the funeral service, the widow approached the minister of music and said, "I'm so sorry. In my grief I wasn't thinking clearly. His favorite song was, 'When They Ring Those Golden Bells.'"

A Difficult Interim

After serving so many churches as interim pastor, I developed a checklist to determine ahead of acceptance if a particular church would prove to be a difficult interim. A church is a difficult interim pastorate:

When all the church vans have gun racks.

When the church staff consists of pastor, minister of education, minister of music, minister of youth, and psycho-pastor.

When the church has an ATM machine in the lobby.

When the church's welcome packet contains a pledge card for the current budget and a warning letter from the deacon chairman.

When the choir wears leather robes.

When the pastor's salary in the budget is listed as "defense spending."

When the Lord's Supper observance is advertised as a "two-drink minimum."

When ushers ask, "smoking or non-smoking?"

When the pastor search committee includes persons with names like: Scarface, Grizzly, Butch, Bonnie and Clyde.

When the church marquee advertises, "Home of the 9 percent tithe.

When the worship bulletin ends with, "We have met to worship, we depart to sin."

When a big argument breaks out in the men's adult Sunday

School class over the feeding of the 5,000—were the two fish bass or catfish?

When opening day of deer season is low attendance day.

When members grumble about Noah allowing coyotes on the ark.

When your meeting with the interim committee is called a "wine-and-cheese gathering."

When the nickname of the minister of music is Little Dictator.

When you notice a truck on the church parking lot with the license tag number—IAM666.

Chapter Nine

My Life with Musicians

I love musicians. While I have zero musical ability, I have been surrounded by musicians most of my life. In addition to family, my life has been enriched by working with some wonderful musicians who have been both sources of laughter as well as partners in it. I have taken great pleasure in showing them the 1991 edition of *The Baptist Hymnal* where the last hymn in the book is number 666.

All in the family—almost

My mother loved music. Since I spent a number of years standing by her in church, I learned to sing alto. Not only did very little room exist in the choir for a boy alto, zero room was available for a boy who was a bad alto. Realizing my voice would not be my musical contribution, my mother purchased a trombone for me and hired a teacher. During the first lesson the teacher showed me the positions on the slide and the different sounds each made. Before the second lesson I learned how to play the trombone and surprised the teacher by playing—by ear—"Whispering Hope" . Then the teacher surprised my mother by packing up his stuff and walking out exclaiming, "I can't teach someone who plays by ear!" Thus came the end of my brief music career. Not to be left without a family musician, my mother turned on my younger brother, Breakfast Bob, who you can hear every Sunday morning on the Internet at *www.solid-gospel.com* and who you can read in his monthly column in *"The Singing News"* magazine.

Showers of something

We often sing "Showers of Blessing" or at least we used to sing it often. During the song portion of one service in a rather old auditorium, something other than blessings began to fall from the ceiling. In snowflake manner little pieces of ceiling acoustics fluttered down between the choir members and Joel Salazar, the minister of music, who was facing the congregation. Folks in the congregation were looking up and snickering. Poor Joel had no idea what was going on, but he kept on singing. Seems someone had been working in the attic during the week. When the air conditioning turned on—during the second verse of a congregational hymn—the loose fluff emerged right on through the vents and fell to the floor below. It was a hot summer day, so the air-conditioning stayed on throughout the service. I felt as though I was preaching in a snowstorm.

Two ministers, two cover-ups, one service

First Baptist Church in Belton, TX, was still using rubber bands to hold the choral music in the choir folders. Its minister of music, Larry Putman, was busily directing congregational singing when one of the rubber bands snapped. It flew as though it had been shot from a rubber-band gun straight into the back of his head. Thinking it to be a bug of some kind, he continued his directing. He simply brought one hand down across the back of his head and never missed a beat.

My cover up was more difficult. An anonymous member provided small flowers each Sunday for the coat lapels of the ministers. On this particular Sunday I made a sweeping gesture announcing, "In the beginning God flung the stars into space." As I did so, my hand brushed into the lapel flower, and sent it sailing into the front row. Quick thinking led to my next line. "Having flung the stars into space, God proceeded to fling the flowers into space, too."

95

A blended worship service

I preached at a small church near the Texas/Oklahoma border and encountered a different kind of blended worship service. Three sets of congregational music were planned before the sermon. After the opening prayer we had "Praise Songs with Cindi" complete with overhead transparencies, taped accompaniment, and live drums. After approximately 10 minutes of this, another prayer was offered. This was followed by 10 minutes of "Singing from the Hymnal" led by Brother Jerry Don and accompanied by Sister Mabel on the slow organ. We then had the offering with piano background music followed by 10 minutes of "Singin' from the Jimmy Davis Quartet Book" led by— are you ready for this?—Brother Bubba. This set included one of my grandfather's favorites, "Life Is Like a Mighty Railroad."

More prayer than that of a minister of music

As the congregational singing ended and the ushers stood at the altar for the offertory prayer, the minister of music began to pray. His mind got a little bit ahead of his mouth and he blurted out, "And Lord, help Dr. Crawford as he sings and the choir as they preach." It is one of the very few times I have ever heard spontaneous laughter break out during a prayer. Eventually, even the minister of music began to laugh. I joined in the laughter, only because it was easier to do than cry. After the choir special I went to the pulpit only to find the minister of music's notebook still lying there. With the audience anticipating a comeback from me, I simply asked, as I held up the notebook, "Is this the song I'm supposed to sing? If so, it's going to take more prayer than can be offered by a minister of music."

Raise my what?

During my interim pastorates I've had the privilege of working with some very talented and committed ministers of music.

Then I've had others . . .. While I appreciate a little background information on a particular hymn I am about to sing, I remember one minister of music who delighted in telling the long versions of the hymn stories. One Sunday this particular expository singer went into a rather lengthy monologue on the story behind the hymn, "Come, Thou Fount of Every Blessing." This wannabee preacher went into great detail to describe what it means in verse two when we sing, "Here I Raise Mine Ebenezer" complete with a brief exegesis of 1 Samuel 7:12 including a definition of *Ebenezer* as a "Stone of Help." It was a wonderful, if a bit wordy, explanation of verse two of the hymn. Then to my amazement this mindless musician instructed us to, "Stand and sing the first and last verses." Not only did I never get to raise mine Ebenezer, I felt like "stoning" a "helpless" minister of music.

O that with yonder sacred what?

One of my very best musician friends is Gerre Joiner. Having moved into the new state-of-the-art worship center, Gerre was excited about putting the texts of the songs on the big overhead screens. Even though some of the songs were quite old and also in the hymnals, we nevertheless had them on the big screens. Not having the budget to purchase the computer program that has the hymn texts already prepared, this church entrusted to one person the task of typing the words from the hymnal into the computer. Even Spell Check won't catch some words. One Sunday as we were singing the words of the great 18th century hymn, "All Hail the Power of Jesus Name," I noticed the teen-age boys on the front rows had stopped singing and started laughing. Since the screens were behind me, I had not seen the misspelled word. Turning quickly to see the source of their amusement, I was horrified to see on the big screens, "O that with yonder sacred *thong* we at His feet may fall!" O what a difference an "r" makes.

Wrong word, right idea

Speaking of Gerre Joiner, we were enjoying some after-meal talk at the dinner table with him and his wife, Jo, and some new friends. My wife surprised and shocked them by asking an innocent question but used the wrong word. One of the meal participants, a delivery room nurse at the nearby hospital, had been recalling a recent case where a baby had been delivered to a rather large woman, who did not know she was pregnant. The woman had arrived at the emergency room complaining of pains—only to discover she was nine-months pregnant and due. After much difficulty, the baby was safely delivered. After this amazing story had been completed, my wife, meaning to use the word "*induced*" asked of the new mother, "Was she '*seduced*'?" To which Gerre concluded, "Well, at least once!"

A silent (and fast) Lord's Supper

In this generation of bells and whistles, platform-roaming preachers, upbeat music, and PowerPoint images, a silent Lord's Supper seems somehow out of place. Besides, most preachers (who make a living with words) have an extremely tough time remaining silent during a one-hour worship service. Nevertheless I decided having a Silent Lord's Supper on the Sunday night before Christmas at a church where I was interim pastor would be a good thing to do. The church had never done this previously but cautiously bought into my idea.

We had the pre-service meeting with the deacons, the majority of whom decided to be somewhere else where they could talk. Then I discovered that both the pianist and the back-up pianist were not going to be present either. So, with a skeleton crew of deacons and a third-string piano player I carefully went over the program.

The pre-service music would end at exactly 6 p.m. With the playing of the first hymn, the deacons would move from the foyer to the front row of the auditorium. Lighting of the Christmas candle would occur. Then we would follow the lead of the pianist throughout the remainder of the service. OK? OK! Much to my surprise the pianist completed the prelude early. with no regard to the time the service began. Since no words could be spoken, I had no choice but to go to the Lord's Supper table. At this point a few of the deacons marched down the aisle to the front row. Others continued to hand out programs in the foyer. Some were not yet back from delivering bread and juice to the nursery workers. As the pianist began to play "The Light of the World is Jesus", the family that was to light the candle arrived. They hurried down to the front, breathing deeply as they lit the candle. Deacons trickled in one at a time.

We then began to observe the Lord's Supper but at a much faster pace than I had ever experienced. The backup to the back-up to the first-string piano player chose to play only the first verse of each hymn and then at a very fast clip. I'm not sure how fast she was playing, but had we been singing, we would have been out of breath by the third song. I tried to signal the minister of music to have her slow down, but he just smiled. I discovered later that to his well-trained musical ear, the pianist was hitting about one wrong key per line. The last thing the minister of music wanted to do was prolong the service.

Twenty-seven minutes after the people had entered the auditorium in silence they left in the same silence. Some had rather bewildered looks on their faces. We had just observed the fastest Lord's Supper in the history of the church. Had we taken an offering they would have felt shortchanged.

Favorite hymn time

A long tradition in churches, especially small, rural ones, is to have a time, usually on Sunday evenings, to sing the favorite hymns of those present. This usually is announced with "Now it's favorite-hymn time. Call out the page number of your favorite hymn. If I know it, I'll lead it. If I don't know it, you get to lead it." At this point, everyone was to laugh politely, even though they had heard this same line dozens of times.

One night in a rural church where I was preaching, the minister of music did this routine and added, "I'll let you be seated; we'll sing the first and last verses of one more song." From the back of the small auditorium came a young voice, "Number 512." To everyone's amazement and the minister of music's embarrassment, "Number 512" was "The Star-Spangled Banner." Of course, we had to stand up again. Also, have you ever sung the last verse of "The Star-Spangled Banner"? The minister of music obviously had not.

Fire in the pulpit; smoke in the balcony
I was preaching at a church in the West Texas panhandle. About half way through the sermon the lights blinked on and off a few times. This generated a flurry of activity in the balcony where the sound techs were sleeping (excuse me, working). More activity than necessary seemed to occur. In a few minutes a man moved down the stairway from the balcony to the lower floor to my left. He walked between the congregation and the pulpit. (We were on TV, so I'm sure this made for interesting viewing.) Then he whispered in the ear of the minister of music, who was seated on the front row to my right. As I continued the sermon, the man walked back between the congregation and me, rather than taking the closer stairway to my right. Then I saw two men in uniforms walking in the balcony. I decided to preach on anyway. I concluded the sermon, prayed, offered the invitation, and we had an announcement or two, followed by the benediction and dismissal.

When I asked the minister of music what had happened he told me the man whispered in his ear—"The attic above the balcony is filled with smoke and it is beginning to come into the balcony. If we'd don't find a source within five minutes we're calling the fire department and will need to evacuate the auditorium." Well, it turned out to be electrical wires causing the smoke. I've always heard where there is smoke, there is fire. I assume the only fire that night was in the pulpit.

Right song, wrong sermon

During my interim pastorates I've served with many ministers of music and worship leaders. Mark Borum was one of my favorites. On one occasion, when someone else was preaching, Mark planned the music for the service without knowing the guest preacher's topic. The sermon title was "The Evils of Gossiping." The last song before the sermon? "I Love to Tell the Story." Mark also told me of the 250-pound soprano who sang "I'll Fly Away," followed by the organ offertory, "It Took a Miracle." I'm not so sure that was a true story, but it could have been.

For all the wrong reasons

Another of my favorite ministers of music is Ronny Barner. Shortly after Ronny retired, he had the following humbling experience. Ronny said. "We all go through a transitional period in our lives as we become *bona fide* senior adults but think we are much younger. I was coming out of Luby's Cafeteria one day. Two lovely young ladies were approaching the entrance. I could tell they were looking and talking about me. You know the feeling when someone puts their hand up to their mouth and says something to someone while looking at you. I had on a new suit and had just returned from my hairdresser. I really felt good about this. Those young ladies were talking about me! Something about me had caught their eye. It put a spring in my step as I walked to my car singing 'Oh Happy

Day.' When I started to open my car door, I looked down and saw my Luby's napkin tucked into my waist hanging all the way down to my knees. Yes, they were looking at me all right. But it was for all the wrong reasons."

With a "g" or not?

Technology is nice when it works. I enjoy singing from the big screens. I know it sounds better to the musicians than when we used to sing with our heads down in a hymn book. However, sometimes not all the letters make it on the screen. While I was serving the second time as interim pastor at First Baptist Church in Lawton, OK, one Sunday we were singing the invitation hymn, "Take My Life, and Let it Be". I looked up at the screen and wanted to burst into laughter but couldn't because this was the invitation hymn. We sang verse two, "Take my feet, and let them be swift and beautiful for Thee; take my voice and let me sing . . .." The problem was the letter "g" did not make it on the screen, so had we sung the words as they were on the screen, we would have sung, "Take my voice, and let me sin." In retrospect, minister of music Tom Willoughby did know the people better than I did. Maybe that's the way he meant to sing it.

Wrong bird call

Speaking of Tom Willoughby, one Sunday morning at the First Baptist Church in Lawton, OK, I was preaching on Matthew 6:25-26. When I got to the part about the "birds of the air", I had arranged for a brief video of many different kinds of birds. Tom thought the bird video was to be on the screen earlier than it actually was, so he sent a text message to the technicians in the control room, "Bird video." In a few seconds he received a reply—"What bird video?" Beginning to panic, Tom sent a second text message, "The bird video for this part of the sermon. The second reply read, "Who is this?" While the bird video appeared on the screen right on que, Tom was busily trying to turn off his cell phone.

Spell check puzzle

Then I'll tell the story of the forever-to-remain-nameless minister of music who listed me in the Sunday morning worship bulletin as: "Sermon—Dr. Dan Crossword." I was puzzled how that happened and even more why he blamed Spell Check for the mistake. Nevertheless the sermon came "Across" well and I sat "Down" with yet another story connected to that same nameless musician.

Chapter Ten

World Travels

As I write this I have been privileged to travel and minister in more than 56 countries, with several more already on the itinerary by the time this book goes to print. Three times I have departed from home and flown completely around the world. This means I have literally laughed my way around the world. World travel has its own brand of humor, as evidenced by the following incidents.

The Hamburg Hamburger

Hamburg, Germany, a beautiful city of two million situated on the North Sea, is the birthplace of the hamburger. So what does one do when in Hamburg but look for a hamburger? The first few people I asked for directions to the nearest good hamburger place said, "McDonalds." I seldom eat at McDonald's in the U.S. I sure had no intentions of being in the birthplace of the hamburger and eating a Big Mac. So, I continued to ask. Finally a bellhop at our hotel directed me to Jones' Bar & Grill, located just a few blocks away. While "Jones" didn't have much of a German ring to it, it did sound better than McDonald's. Sure enough, Jones' Bar & Grill actually looked German with many beer signs decorating the establishment. The waiter, having traveled in Canada, actually spoke some English. The menu was mostly in German until on page three the word "Hamburger" appeared. Just under it was "Hamburger mit cheese bis salat." I ordered the Cheeseburger and salad with a side order of curly fries and a soft drink. I had already been in Germany long enough to anticipate disappointment in the soft drink. It would likely be served in a small glass without ice. A refill would cost the same as the original. I had much higher hopes for the cheeseburger. Germans make great fries. The salad would be a bonus.

Anticipation gave way to major disappointment when the cheeseburger arrived. First glance revealed something purple hanging out of the bun. A look at the meat caused a brief flashback to my days of eating in the college dining hall. What was the white stuff in the patty? And where was the salad? A closer look found the salad inside the cheeseburger bun — purple lettuce, green lettuce, one slice of tomato, a slice of onion, and one thing more. Of all the audacity! Someone had placed a cucumber in my cheeseburger. And the salad dressing? A poor imitation of Thousand Island had been poured over the salad. This created a very soggy bun.

First bite caused a very bad salad-dressing stain on my pants and an even worse taste in my mouth. As the soggy bun fell apart in my hands, I struggled through half of the mushy cheeseburger before surrendering. I could eat no more. The minute soft-drink glass had long since been emptied. I dumped a load of Catsup on the curly fries, dreamed of McDonalds, and gave thanks for the evolution of the hamburger.

Never Mind, Lord

I had accompanied a prayer team to Benin, West Africa. After two days of prayerwalking in the 118-degree heat, we were walking down a dirt road through a small African village when I heard a most unusual prayer. We had prayed for nearly everything we could think of to pray for in that village, but we continued to walk. Just then we turned a corner and faced a huge, white marble statue. We had no idea who the statue was, nor could anyone in the group read the French inscription.

Maybe it was the heat, maybe the jet-lag, maybe the frustration of hearing the same prayer phrases so often, but whatever the motivation, a team member prayed, "Lord, I pray for this statue . . . ." During the long pause that followed I found myself wondering what was next. What is the proper prayer for a white stone statue? Finally, the frustrated team member continued, "Oh, never mind Lord. I can't think of anything to pray for that dumb statue." Ever wonder if God has a sense of humor? Surely God at least smiled on hearing that statue prayer.

The 12 churches of Revelation

Sometimes you teach your heart out and no one listens—or at least it seems that way. I accompanied a group of missionaries and ministers on a trip to visit the sites of the seven churches of Asia Minor, better known as the seven churches addressed by John in the book of Revelation. I was the Bible teacher and offered background information on the churches situated in the ancient cities of Ephesus, Smyrna, Pergamos, Thyatira, Sardis, Philadelphia, and Laodicea. After a week of teaching and answering questions, the group had its final meal together before returning to the U.S.

At the conclusion of the meal the group leader made a few positive remarks about my teaching and presented me with a wonderful book—*Ephesus: Ruins and Museum*. Besides the signatures of all participants inside the front cover, the group leader had written this inscription on behalf of the team, "Thank you for making the 12 churches come alive to us." The scary thing was that as each missionary/minister on the team signed the book, not one of these learned folks had corrected the number of churches in the inscription.

Up above my head

During a sabbatical leave from Southwestern Baptist

Seminary, I taught for a semester at the Bible Seminary in Bonn, Germany. On our arrival at the campus seminarians helped move us into our small efficiency apartment. They apologized that it was situated under the school's library. I assured them that it would not be the first time German theology had been over my head. Having been on the road for several weeks, I needed to find a German barber and get a haircut. In my best, slow, deliberate English I explained what kind of haircut I desired. I think I miscommunicated somewhere. Now, not only did I have German theology above my head, I had very little hair on the top of my head. In addition, when I left the barber-shop without tipping the barber, he mispronounced my name when he said, "Thank you, Mr. Dummkoft."

A sabbatical visit with a German doctor

I had spent several weeks hauling heavy luggage up and down railway stairs and wondered why the Germans couldn't fix their escalators. Somewhere in the former East Germany near Berlin I pulled a muscle or something. "Surely, just an aggravated old athletic injury," I thought, although I couldn't remember ever having an athletic injury in this exact location. I e-mailed my doctor in Fort Worth, confident that he would say what he always says, "Let's watch it a few days and see what happens"—giving me comfort and making the pain go away. However, he surprised me with, "See an English-speaking doctor immediately." Thus, began a great adventure.

A lengthy search produced Dr. Angela (her "very-German" last name is withheld to protect her medical practice) who spoke some English. A seminary student was recruited to accompany me to the doctor's office. As humiliating as it was to go to a German doctor's office for the first time, I had to endure the most thorough hernia exam I'd ever had—from a woman doctor. This may have been my imagination, but I thought her certificate on the wall read, "East German School of Gestapo Medicine." Nevertheless, after a reference to my body being "kaput" her verdict was "no hernia . . . yet, but don't lift any more heavy luggage." "Are you kidding?" I replied. "We only take heavy luggage when we travel." Very interesting, but not funny! Dr. Angela assured me that if the pain continued, I should call her immediately. That of itself kept me from lifting any more heavy luggage.

On the way back to the reception desk Dr. Angela announced my condition—"*diagnosen leisten-hernie!*" loud enough for the entire waiting room, including my student accompanist, to hear. Not only did my student accompanist explain my condition to me, but he also shared with everyone he knew. By the time my four-month sabbatical leave was completed, I had a full-blown hernia and returned to Fort Worth for surgery. At least I now understand why some of my colleagues spend their sabbatical leave in a remote mountain cabin writing books.

Remembering Dr. Angela

Several months after my experience with Dr. Angela, I had an occasion to remember her. I was enduring my first colonoscopy. Other than diverticulosis, I was fine—or at least I was when I completely got over the side effects of the scope. As I was lying on the table in my birthday suit, with my wrong end sticking up in the air and the nurse patting me on the cheek (no, the other one) and the doctor saying cute things like, "This is not hurting me one bit," I thought of Dr. Angela in Bonn, Germany. Immediately I felt better about my surroundings and circumstances. Nevertheless, if your doctor ever says anything that even remotely sounds like *colonoscopy*, take my advice and run as fast as you can in the opposite direction.

Olympic Games—British style

During the 2000 Summer Olympic Games we were in Europe. We had to rely on receiving our Olympic TV coverage via Eurosport—a 24-hour sports station out of London. When not covering the Olympics, Eurosport normally covers such exciting sporting events as cricket, rugby, and table tennis. By the end of the sixth day of Olympic coverage we had yet to hear any mention of baseball, softball, volleyball, boxing, and men's or women's basketball. One slight reference to soccer occurred. A brief glimpse of a women's beach volleyball game between Germany and Brazil was given. We did get the news that five horses had fallen in the equestrian events. However, we only saw a brief videotape of one fall—that one was where the rider's pelvis was broken. Actually this video was shown several times in slow motion. We watched hours of swimming, mixed with judo, weightlifting, fencing, and a few segments of gymnastics.

The announcers ("That was a real cracker of a race!") were so anti-American that they took a commercial break during the opening ceremonies when the USA team entered the coliseum. One commentator described the end of a close swimming race as, "She finished like a liner docking." The swimmer in lane eight was described as "an outside smoker." Another Brit announcer summed up the achievements of a gold medalist with, "She put the cat in the middle of the pigeons." Why can't they use normal phrases such as "The ducks are on the pond," or "He had his bell rung," or "She performed within herself." In the midst of hearing about all of the USA swimmers from The University of Texas, my wife remarked, "We haven't met an Aggie since we've been in Europe." Now, that was a thought worth pondering.

Pray for whose cow?

I took a prayer team to the small country of Macau to pray

with missionaries there during ceremonies marking the transfer of their country from Portuguese rule to Chinese rule. Prior to this trip I had asked the church where I was serving as interim pastor to please remember me in prayer during my visit to Macau. On my return a grandmother in the church told me of the mealtime prayer when the "amen" was followed by her grandson's exclamation, "We forgot to pray for Dr. Crawford's cow!" It took the family several minutes to determine what the child meant. He kept repeating, "Dr. Crawford asked us to pray for his cow." I'm just glad someone in the family was listening when I made the request to pray for Macau.

An Honest Prayer

On the last day of a three-week prayer journey around the world my colleague, Bob Garrett, was called on to offer the blessing at breakfast. Five grown men more accustomed to living with their wives had lived together 24-hours a day for 21 days. We had survived a week in China and the stress of carefully guarding our every word for fear of saying something illegal. We had endured a week among the poverty stricken of India. We had now completed a week in a part of the Middle Eastern world, where once again any misspoken word could spell trouble. We had prayed our way through varied circumstances. We had enjoyed and endured each other's irritable habits. We had laughed and cried together. Now we were tired and homesick. On this final morning Bob dutifully thanked God for the food and the previous night's rest. Then he added, "And Lord, please get us home before we kill each other."

Don't just add an "A" to the end of the word

I met a missionary in a Caribbean country who told of describing to a group of natives his wife's hobby. She was into mountain-climbing. She was so skilled at this adventure that she often climbed without a safety rope. He had learned that when in doubt, one can often add an "a" to the end of an English word and make a Spanish word out of it. The missionary meant to say of his wife, "She often climbs without her rope" but could not remember the Spanish word for rope. Undaunted, he simply added an "a" to rope and make it "*ropa*," the Spanish word for clothes. He was especially pleased when the natives showed heightened interest in this hobby.

Selected for What?

The Sunday before I spoke in a church in Mexico City was deacon-ordination Sunday. A secretarial mistake still had many of the congregation laughing and a few deacons getting over shock. The secretary had asked the pastor what to put on the front of the Sunday bulletin. He said, "Just put Acts 6:3." She asked, "Do you want the verse?" He said, "No, just the Scripture reference. Put some flowers or something around it to make it look nice."

Of course, this is the verse often used at deacon ordinations that speaks of selecting seven good men to serve. However, she misunderstood the scripture reference. The Sunday bulletin proclaimed Acts 16:3.

The church nearly lost one deacon before the ordination when during the song service he looked up the bulletin scripture in his Bible and read about Paul wanting to take Timothy along with him, "*so he circumcised him.*"

A doctor that can't help much

For several days we had been visiting in the home of a young missionary couple in Eastern Europe. Their 4-year-old daughter had adopted us quickly—perhaps out of missing her own grandparents. After hearing her parents and others refer to me as "Dr. Crawford" she finally asked me, "So are you really a doctor?" I assured her that I was, to which she responded, "Well, I have this cough." After a brief period of controlled laughter, I told her I wasn't really a medical doctor that could assist her with recovery from her cold.

The next time the missionary mother referred to me as "doctor," the 4-year old quickly corrected her mother. "Don't call him a doctor any more. He can't help us much."

Offerings to professor buddha

For many years I took a group of 10 seminary students each summer to Vancouver, British Columbia, Canada, as a part of an urban evangelism practicum. Because of the great cultural diversity in Vancouver, many temples and other sites of world religions are there. During the week we would visit these sites. One particular year an unusual event happened at the Buddhist Temple. One of the Buddhist Monks came out and asked to speak to the leader of our group. I introduced myself as the professor of the class. He graciously offered to answer any questions the students had. Of course, many questions arose. A series of questions centered on the fresh fruit placed at the base of each statue of Buddha. The answer was that the fruit was placed there by individuals in respect and as an offering in hopes of gaining Buddha's favor. Then someone asked about a bottle of Mazola Oil that had been placed in the midst of the fruit. The Monk laughed and explained that someone apparently had no fresh fruit to offer, so the person simply gave what he or she had. Eventually someone asked who could become a Buddha, since several Buddhas were in this temple. The monk replied that such an honor was not difficult and that, "Even your professor could become a Buddha". We had not even made it back to our van in the parking lot before I was being called "Dr. Buddha" and "Professor Buddha," a practice that continued for the remainder of the week. Two weeks after the practicum the students had to submit a reflection paper evaluating their experiences in Vancouver. To my amazement when I arrived at my office on the morning the papers were due, I found 10 papers lined up across my floor, nine of which were accompanied with fresh fruit. What accompanied the 10th paper? You guessed it—a bottle of Mazola Oil.

Chapter Eleven

Retirement—The Beat (and the Laughter) Goes On

Robert Browning wrote, "Grow old along with me, the best of life is yet to be." Having advanced several years into retirement, I would like to paraphrase that famous line. "Grow old along with me, the funniest experiences of life are yet to be." Or maybe I should paraphrase another rather famous line, "the closer I get to the end, the funnier life becomes." I'm really not sure how I lived this long when I consider that in my younger years:

I slept in a baby crib that was covered with bright colored lead-based paint.

I never saw a medicine bottle with a childproof lid.

I ran through the house while I held scissors.

I rode my bicycle everywhere and wore no helmet.

I rode in cars that had no seat belts and no air bags.

I drank water from the garden hose rather than from a bottle.

When I did drink from a bottle, it was often the same bottle from which friends drank.

Do dogs laugh?

Miss Belle is the same long-red-haired miniature daschund that has lived with us for more than 15 years. Fulke Greville, a minor Elizabethan poet, dramatist, and statesman, once said, "Man is the only creature endowed with the power of laughter." Don't tell that to Miss Belle.

You know you're retired when . . .

Shortly after I retired, a friend sent me the following list. You know you're retired when:

Everything begins to hurt and what doesn't hurt, doesn't work.

You join a health club but never go.

You decide to procrastinate but never get around to it.

Your mind begins to make contracts that your body can't meet.

You know all the answers, but no one asks you the questions anymore.

The little old gray-haired lady you help walk across the street is your wife.

You no longer have an irrational fear of aging. It is now rational.

It's too late to get in shape. Being out of shape is now a part of your personality.

It's now too late to get rich. Why invest for old age when you're already old?

They play your music in elevators.

You exercise early in the morning before your brain realizes what you are doing.

You realize that for every 15 minutes of exercise you get, you add one minute to your life. This will eventually enable you to live in a nice nursing home at $5,000.00 per month.

You are told that the advantage of walking every day is so when you die, they'll say, "Well, he looks good, doesn't he."

The Fort Worth Cats

One of the great things about living and retiring in Fort Worth is the return of the minor league baseball team—the Fort Worth Cats. The Cats had a notable history as an earlier member of the Texas League and producer of many major-league stars. Having grown up watching the Houston Buffaloes play the Cats in the old Texas League, I was an eager season-ticket holder. I will never forget the opening game of the new Cats' first season. Or should I say, I will never forget the guy who sat next to me during that game. Wow! Was I ever lucky?

No sooner had I sat down in my seat than the guy informed me that he was at the game because he and the Cats' starting pitcher, Jose Guzman, were best friends. Knowing that Guzman had won 80 games in eight seasons with the Chicago Cubs and the Texas Rangers, I guess I looked somewhat skeptical. Silly me. Sensing that I was unimpressed, my new friend continued, "Me and him played on the same team last summer." The fact that Guzman hurt his arm in 1994 and never pitched professional baseball again until this summer caused my response to not register a very high score on my new friend's ego scale. Undaunted, he pressed on, "Guzie pitched a no hitter last summer in a tournament in Cooperstown, NY, and the other guy pitched a one-hitter and we won." "Let me guess," I ventured. "You got the one hit to win the game." "Yeah, that's right!" Unfortunately my comment was falsely interpreted by my neighbor as interest. This caused him to continue talking. "I brought my boy here to the game so he could see Guzie pitch." Unhuh! I had never heard Jose Guzman called "Guzie" before, but then I had never been one of his "best friends" either.

When the fact that I was not interested became obvious, my row buddy turned to repeat the same story to the folks who had just arrived to sit behind us. After a few innings I risked the start-up of another conversation by asking, "These your season tickets?" I feared that the short, home-game schedule had just gotten longer. Dumb me, I should have guessed. "Nah, Guzie sent me these so my boy could see him pitch tonight." Yeah, right! I'm not sure whether it was a sign of maturity or if I was tired, but I resisted the impulse to try to top his story. Long-time baseball legend and former Cat great Bobby Bragan and I had dedicated the new baseball stadium at Pan American University (now University of Texas, Pan American) once upon a time— before my new friend knew which end of a bat to grip. But that's another story.

A fast ball to the forehead - no pain, no gain
Retirement years bring an interesting assortment of ills. Having aggravated a lower disk problem in my back, I was sent to physical therapy. Most of the exercises were challenging and fun. One particularly interesting exercise was performed while I was seated on a large rubber ball. First I would bounce for three minutes and then march for three minutes. I assumed that both of these activities were designed to strengthen the muscles in my lower back. Then, while still balancing on the rubber ball, I would throw a smaller rubber ball from above my head with both hands into a small, trampoline-appearing object. The ball of course would bounce off the trampoline and return to me. In throwing and catching the ball I assumed again that I was strengthening the lower-back muscles. All was going well until the day my therapist gave me a six-pound ball.

I never was real good at physics. Either I failed to listen or was absent the day the physics teacher covered the return speed of a large rubber ball thrown into a trampoline-looking object. While I would sometimes make an errant throw, causing the ball to return to the right or left of my head, this time I made a perfect throw. The heavy ball bounced off the trampoline and returned at a rather rapid speed, directly at my forehead. With my once lightening-quick reflexes, I moved my hands to the front of my glasses to catch the ball. Apparently on the same day the physics teacher discussed the return speed of a rubber ball, the subject of force at which a returning rubber ball hits one's hands was also discussed. And I missed it. I missed the lecture, not the ball. Fortunately I caught the ball. Unfortunately the force of the returning ball drove my hands into my forehead and my thumbnail into my scalp. Somehow I retained my balance on the large rubber ball, but as I began to bleed I realized how much physical therapy and physics have in common. My back is better and my forehead has stopped bleeding. No pain, no gain.

A game of Play Like

As you age, some childhood games return to your memory. I called the phone company to get information and possibly order a much faster line for computer use. After I asked several questions repeatedly, I was satisfied that I could get the service needed for only $29.95 per month. I was assured that the installation fee would be waived. I was told they would send me everything in the mail to self-install. I was further assured that I would not have to wire anything in or hook anything up. "Just pop in the disk and follow the directions. I did it myself," the sales girl said. "Is this all of the fees?" I asked. "Yes, sir!" was the reply. "So, I get the package in the mail and the next thing I get is a monthly bill for $29.95. Is that correct?" I asked. "Yes, sir!" was the reply once again.

I was switched to a supervisor to double-check my order before getting my order number. This always makes me wonder about the expertise of the first person with whom I dealt. "Sir, you're monthly fee will be $34.95." "Whoa! What happened to the $29.95?" "Oh, that's if you already have all of our service options and you do not." "So" I asked, "If I have all of the services, I get this faster package and the services for $29.95?" "No, the service you want is $29.95 and the optional services are extra. When these extras are added to your monthly phone bill, they total approximately $15.00 per month, so you are better off keeping the services you have and paying the $34.95 per month for the faster service."

Now I was greatly relieved to know I was going to be better off this way. "Now Sir, the normal installation fee is $149.95 and we are waiving $100 of that, so your installation fee is only $49.95. That will be added to your next phone bill." "Time out!!! I thought, since you were mailing me the self-installation kit, there was no installation fee?" "Well, we have to charge some fee."

Oh, now I understand. How stupid of me to assume that the installation of a self-installation kit would be free. "Just out of curiosity," I inquired, "can we go over again what is in the self-installation kit?" "Sure, there is the external modem and . . .." "Wait right there. Does that have to be hooked up?" "Yes, sir, but anyone can do it."

Oh, that's good. Maybe my granddaughter can do it for me. "Never mind, let me be sure I understand ALL of the charges— $49.95 installation fee for the self-installation kit plus $34.95 per month for the use of the faster service since I don't have all the optional services. Is that it?"

"Yes, sir, plus the shipping and handling charges of $12.95, but that will be added to your next bill." "Let me guess the next one—is all of this subject to tax? "Yes sir."

"Miss, when you were a child did you ever play a game called 'Play Like?' "Yes sir." "Then, why don't you just *play like* I never called."

What a difference an "L" makes

Annual physical exams become routine in retirement. I went in to such an exam feeling fine and anticipating no surprises. All was well until the results of the blood test came back. The nurse left a message with my wife. I was to call the doctor first thing the next morning and be put on a powerful medication immediately for high LDL cholesterol. For many years I had received a low HDL cholesterol reading, so this was quite a surprise. I'd never had high LDL. When I looked up this medication on the Internet, I discovered awful side effects, even unto death. Plus it required close monitoring for the first few months of usage. I could not be monitored because of an upcoming trip to Eastern Europe. So I saw my European-tour plans deteriorating before my eyes. Could I even make the scheduled trip to Vancouver, Canada, in two days? Needless to say, it was a long night. Sometime during the night I decided that I would not call the doctor but go to his office at 7:30 a.m. and wait until I could see him. I was developing many questions.

Around 5 a.m. I finally gave up all attempts to sleep and got up. At 7:30 a.m. I was in the doctor's cold, little, patient-waiting room with an extremely high-blood-pressure reading. I was a nervous wreck. I wondered what the future held.

Finally the doctor entered and said. "So you want to talk with me in person about your test results? It's like I told you six months ago, if your HDL continues to be low, we're going to treat it."

"Excuse me Doc. What was the LDL reading?" I asked somewhat confused. "Oh, that one was great. Let me see— 75," answered the doctor. Anything under 100 is great for LDL.

"So I don't have high cholesterol?" I replied. "Nope! Just the same low HDL reading you've had ever since I've been treating you," Doc said.

"So I'm not going to die?" I asked.

"What?" he replied. "Never mind," I said. "Thanks for your time. Enjoy the $30.00 co-pay"

"OK" the doctor answered. "We'll have to get together sometime over coffee and discuss something non-medical like reformed theology."

"In that case," I said, "you'll owe me a $30 co-pay. See ya."

What a difference an "L" makes.

Advantage, grandson!

Amazing! I have resisted sharing grandkid stories almost to the end of the book. Well, not so amazing. Grandkids usually accompany retirement years. Nevertheless, our family including grandkids was eating at Luby's Cafeteria one evening. The approximately-college-age waiter seemed especially interested in our older-than-she-looks 14-year-old granddaughter. In fact with my tea glass sitting on the table empty, he made several trips by our table and asked our granddaughter, "Do you need some more Sprite, Ma'am?" The smarter-than-he-looks 2-1/2-year old grandson observed all of this while he finished off a bowl of corn. The waiter passed by again and asked, "Can I get anything else for you?" looking especially at the granddaughter. As we were all politely declining any further service, the grandson exclaimed, "I need some more corn!" Seeking to make a good impression on the granddaughter while working on his tip, the waiter rushed to get another bowl of corn. We all sat patiently sipping on our drinks and me sucking on my ice cubes while the grandson slowly ate his second bowl of corn. In a few minutes the semi-silence of the cafeteria was broken as the grandson yelled, "Hey man!" The now-more-than-ever-interested-waiter rushed over only to hear from the grandson, "I need some cake!" We weren't sure, but it seemed the grandson had learned how to use the granddaughter's beauty to his own advantage.

Inherited kitchen manners

The same grandson at age 4 was playing with the little girl next door when he got hungry. He proceeded to go into the kitchen and tell the girl's mother, "When you have a guest in your home, you normally offer then something to eat!" Whereupon, she cooked him some macaroni and cheese. Wonder where he got those kitchen manners?

Disciples at the dance

When my granddaughter attended her first dance at her Christian high school, she heard the school principal remind the students, "Leave enough room between you and your dancing partner for Jesus." Her father, who happened to be a reluctant chaperone, walked over to Whitney and said, "You need to add a few disciples between you and your partner."

You can go through home again

Thomas Wolfe wrote a book entitled *You Can't Go Home Again*. While that may be true, the fact that you can go *through* home again is also true. Early in this book I stated concerning my collegiate days, "Student days are the greatest days of all." That's one reason I'm thrilled beyond measure in my retirement years to be asked to serve as an officer on the board of directors for the alumni association of my alma mater, Howard Payne University. I am so glad the university did not do any background checks before asking me to serve! I am now going *through* home again. It is an unexplainable experience to walk around campus again and see:

The tree where I fell asleep one night while "guarding the campus" and the hard ground on to which I fell.

My dorm room whose door opened toward the hallway bathroom, where we tossed cherry bombs at fellow students who were minding their own private business.

The cafeteria where they sometimes had to force-feed the garbage disposal.

The chapel auditorium where I got some of my best sleep.

The library. I always wondered what was actually inside there.

The biology lab where my dissecting of a frog proved why God called me to be a minister and not a surgeon.

The post office—lifeline to next week's social life.

The bookstore—where students bought books and alumni bought everything else.

The women's dorm—field of dreams.

The original men's dorm, where students were prepared for overseas missionary duty—intermittent running water, little heat in the winter, no air-conditioning, rough wooden floors designed to prepare tender young feet for jungle trails and mountain paths, steep, narrow steps to build endurance, snack bar to prepare students for possible food poisoning on the mission field.

The new men's dorm—finally air-conditioning had been installed—no more "sauna sanctuary"!

The gymnasium—exactly why were we forced to run up and down those bleachers?

The Bible building, where my beloved professor, Dr. B.O., would give such impossible exams that getting to the third question before the bell rang was challenging.

The president's office—see earlier bonfire and outhouse story.

Chapter Twelve

Shared Laughter

One thing that is better than laughter is shared laughter. Once I started sharing my stories, I was amazed how many people had stories they wanted to share with me. This final chapter is a collection of their stories. So for now you can cease laughing at and with me. Join me in laughing with someone else.

"To Him Who Loved us and Washed Us . . ."

For 22 years I directed a program at Southwestern Baptist Seminary that sent student-preachers out during spring break to preach revival meetings in small churches situated outside the Bible Belt. Brandon Boatner returned with a story about his first attempt to baptize a new believer. Brandon said, "During the revival I was really nervous about doing my first-ever baptism. When the time was getting really close, I grew very fearful of slipping up, so I decided to jot some notes on my arm. We had practiced the baptism. I knew my left arm would be bracing the lady's back and I would be able to see what I wrote but she wouldn't. After putting on a large white robe I wrote, 'with your public profession of faith, I now baptize you in . . ..' The plan was fool proof until things didn't go as planned. On entering the water the woman turned around opposite of what we practiced. Knowing she could now see the writing, I quickly dunked my arm under the water and washed off my notes. I didn't forget my wording and the baptism went off great. I certainly will never forget my first baptism."

Hot water resurrection

One of the less obvious joys of serving as an interim pastor is meeting outstanding, younger men who are called to be pastors of the churches you have just served as interim. Such a one was Kevin McCallon. Kevin shared this great baptism story with me: "My first pastorate was in a lower Alabama county seat town among a great people worshiping in a fine sanctuary that had an added baptistery. The baptistery was a cast-iron tub placed directly behind the choir, high enough for all to see, with only one entrance to the side, and equipped with the heavy felt drapes of many past motion-picture theaters. An even later addition was a heater that was a prong dipped into the trough. It was equipped with a thermostat that had to be turned off each Sunday morning before baptism to keep it from getting too hot.

One memorable Easter Sunday we planned for baptism. As fate would have it, I forgot to turn off the heater. The service was starting when we opened the side door to enter the water from the side and saw steam rising off the water. I quickly checked and found it wasn't too hot to use but was more like a bath/spa than a baptistery. The young girl I was baptizing said she still wanted to proceed, so we plunged in, closed the door, and awaited the right moment in the service. As the music started, I began to notice the heat was making me a bit woozy. I never expected that opening the curtain would release a mighty cloud into the sanctuary! The crowd let out an audible, 'whoa!' and looked on what seemed like a Broadway-produced baptism heaven itself would have been proud of. I usually ask candidates if they believe that God could one day raise them from the dead as Jesus Himself was raised. On this day the words came out over the sound system from my mouth as, 'Molly, have you been raised from the dead?'

" 'Yes!' She replied with joy. The crowd applauded as she went under the water and back to her feet smiling!

"I believe all went home smiling that day, not only because Christ is risen indeed, but because they'd gotten to personally see one who said she'd already been through it!"

Hello God . . . my name is Ed

Translation stories are so numerous they could easily fill a book unto themselves. A missionary friend in China related the following account to me. A new missionary, still in the very early days of language study, had to make an emergency trip back to the United States for the funeral of his father. After the service he had remained for a few days to assist his mother with details and was still at home on Sunday. This afforded him an opportunity to visit his home church for the Sunday morning worship service. At the conclusion of the service, the pastor recognized the missionary and asked him to lead in closing prayer. The pastor added, "Since you are a missionary to China, we'd love to hear you pray in Chinese." Momentary panic at not yet being very fluent in Mandarin quickly gave way to creativity. Thus the missionary "prayed" in the only Chinese words he had learned, "Hello God. How are you today? My name is Ed. I am fine, thank you. One, two, three, four, five, six, seven, eight, nine , 10. Good night. Amen." After the service many people expressed to Ed that having him home and hearing that beautiful Chinese prayer was wonderful. Then an elderly couple stepped up to greet him. "We are retired missionaries from China. It's so good to meet you. By the way, we loved your prayer. Best wishes in your continued language study."

Many are cold, few are frozen

My faculty colleague Al Fasol shared the following story from the life of a long-ago professor: "The professor was invited to preach at a church more than 100 miles from his home. Since he had only one car, he asked a student if he could ride with him. The student was pastor not far from where the professor would preach. The student had to leave on a Saturday night. Arrangements were made for someone to pick up the professor at an appointed site where 'two pine trees stand out in a field not far from the highway'. Arrangements were made to meet the professor's host at 6:30 p.m. Did I mention the date was in January? The student and professor arrived at the twin pines. A bitterly cold north wind was blowing, but no one came for the professor. The student apologized because he had to get to a youth event at his church and had no choice but to let the professor out in the cold. With only twin pines for shelter, the professor waited nearly 45 minutes before his host arrived. As the professor rushed to get into the warm cab of the pickup, his host said, 'I sure am glad you are here. I didn't want to have to wait in this cold.'"

A couple of missionary stories

Bob Cullen, now retired, was a career missionary to Thailand. He shared with me the following two stories from his days in Thailand:

"After our arrival on the field I was asked to preach at the first annual meeting of missionaries in Thailand. I had not been preaching 10 minutes when I lost the attention of two of the missionaries on the front row. I was very distracted by their lack of attentiveness to my sermon. When I finished and started down from the pulpit, they both said, 'Go the other way!' I looked behind me. Not three feet from where I was standing was a cobra. That was what had their attention. But as I walked away I thought, 'Don't they know that cobras can strike from greater distance than that?'

"Then one Sunday in Thailand I was showing a new missionary couple a church they might attend. After church I invited the pastor to be my guest for lunch. I also said he could ask someone to join us. He turned and announced to the church that I was taking the entire church to lunch. I quickly ran to the departing missionary couple and asked to borrow all the money they had. I'm glad I did, because it took all of mine and all of theirs to pay for the lunch."

Food court fun

My good friend Ray Woodard loves to tell of an experience with a group of college-student, summer missionaries that he was hosting in Vancouver, British Columbia, Canada. The students became especially fond of a local Asian food court. In spite of the unusual sights and smells, the food was inexpensive and the portions were large. However, some of the students occasionally had difficulty eating some of the items. One young man spent the first half of the summer bragging that he could eat anything, regardless of what it looked like or smelled like. One particular day Ray arrived at the food court early for his meeting with the students. He purchased some small pork strips and was eating them when the students arrived. "What's that" asked the bold 'I-can-eat-anything' student?" Ray simply extended the plate to the student who took a pork strip and put it in his mouth. At about the third chew, Ray responded to the student's question, "Monkey brains!" The student was last seen moving rather quickly toward the nearest men's restroom.

Baptism shorts

Dr. Jerry Winfield, a good friend and former pastor to my brother, Breakfast Bob, shared the following: "I had always heard about the feeling of 'freedom' in preaching. I just assumed that it had something to do with the work of the Holy Spirit in the preparation and delivery of the message. Well, I learned a whole new meaning of 'freedom' in the pulpit following a baptismal service. Early in my ministry I decided to not use waders in the baptistery. Several reasons lead to this decision: waders were too hot, too cumbersome, and on occasion when least expected, they leaked (that's another story). I simply undressed, put on pants, shirt, and disposable tie and then my robe. When I say undressed, I mean undressed right down to removing my underwear. One Sunday in my haste to get on my baptismal clothes, I forgot to take off my boxers. After baptizing several candidates, I went back to my stall to change back into my preaching regalia. Lo and behold, I was wearing soaking wet shorts! I had neglected to remove this important item of clothing before taking the plunge. Since there was little I could do at the time and little time to do it, I simply removed the wet 'drawers,' dried myself off, got dressed, and went into the service to preach. Needless to say, that day I experienced a whole new sense of 'freedom' in the pulpit. I don't remember what I preached, how I preached, or how the people responded. I do remember discovering that there are simply too many other distractions for the preacher to have to deal with this one. For those of you who just might follow the same practice as me in preparing to baptize, please allow me to give you a helpful hint: an extra pair of underwear hidden away in your desk drawers in not a bad idea at all!"

Seen on the Radio

Ed Hogan was president of the Baptist Student Ministries at the University of Texas when I was the director. He is now a very gifted pastor. He shared this story from an earlier pastorate: "Crockett, TX, has a couple of radio stations. The one I am most familiar with plays country music. They don't do current musicians. They do Hank Williams Sr., Ray Price, and Box Car Willie. Some folks in Crockett think that Waylon, Willie, and the Boys are 'new school.' My first week in Crockett I discovered that my church members had purchased 15 minutes a week for me on the radio—LIVE—every Sunday morning. What they did not tell me was the spot was next to the Church of Christ preacher who did not take too well to Baptists. I quickly learned the peculiar ways of Deep East Texas. A few years into my ministry in Crockett, our church bought three two-minute spots for Monday through Friday. We were nestled between the school-lunch menus, lottery numbers, the weather report, and obituaries. That is prime real estate. One morning I spoke of Little League parents and their overly ambitious ways. I might as well have slapped Uncle Sam and Betty Crocker. Feedback was swift and furious. I reassured the radio owner that in the future I would engage safe topics like religion and politics and avoid hot button topics such as Little League. He seemed relieved. Later that week we were at the grocery store. An elderly lady from a nearby town recognized my voice and said: 'You are Ed Hogan. You are better looking on radio.' She was a 'steel magnolia blue hair' in the best sense of that word. She looked at my wife, Marion, and said: 'Kind of disappointing isn't it?' Marion replied: 'You have no idea!'"

Small-town parades and large-town parades

When Ed Hogan moved from small town Crockett in Deep East Texas to Jersey Village in suburban Houston, his son Matt was 8-years old. He loved Crockett with all of its fishing holes and deer stands. He was a little cynical about moving to the city. Less than a week after arriving Ed and Matt attended the Jersey Village High School Homecoming Parade. Ed related the story: "Matt was delighted that the kids on the floats seemed to recognize us. He was especially excited about the candy thrown his way from the floats. As the parade ended, I took him by the hand and told him it was time to go. He pulled back and argued that the parade was not over. I asked what he meant. Matt replied:

'The parade can't be over! Where are the John Deere tractors? There are always tractors at the end of the parade!!' That was my chance to explain to Matt that there were no tractors because no horses were in the parade. Tractors were always last in Crockett parades because they had the privilege of scooping up the little presents the horses had left behind. Begrudgingly we headed to the car."

Called on the Carpet or on the Green?

The following story was shared with me by seminary colleague Jack Terry: "I came to Southwestern Seminary to teach in the School of Religious Education under the deanship of Joe Davis Heacock. While I was teaching at Hardin-Simmons University in Abilene, TX, I served under a very demanding religion-division chairman. If you were ever called to his office, you were in real trouble. The consequences would not be pleasant. I taught under this kind of administration for three years before moving to the seminary. I had been at Southwestern for about five months when one day at chapel Dr. Heacock caught me and said, 'I'll see you in my office at 2 p.m.' He gave no further explanation nor information. I was panicked. I remembered my three years with the division chairman at Hardin-Simmons University. I hardly knew what I taught to my 11 a.m. class and didn't want anything to eat at noon. My stomach was churning and a bit unsettled. At 2 p.m. I appeared in Dr. Heacock's office where he was signing letters. Without a word he simply motioned for me to sit down. I spent an eternity waiting for him to sign all those letters. Finally when he was finished, he looked up and said, 'Jack, what are you doing this afternoon at 4 p.m.? I have a golf tee time with two other faculty members. We would like for you to be the fourth player. I know you have your clubs and shoes in your car. Can you do that for me?' With a great sigh of relief, I said, 'Yes, I will be happy to do so!' I got out of that office as quickly as I could. I didn't win the round of golf, but I was much calmer playing in the afternoon than I was teaching after the chapel hour."

Revival wardrobe malfunction

The following story comes from long-time friend Judy Davis: "There's nothing new in the world including 'wardrobe malfunctions.' In the early 1950s a visiting evangelist came to the First Baptist Church in Elgin, TX, to hold a week-long revival. Responses to his sermons hadn't been what he hoped for, but he preached his heart out at every service. My paternal grandmother, 'Mama Davis,' was present for every service. On this particular evening she was flanked by my Aunt Ora and Aunt Pearl. Mama Davis had no sense of humor, but Aunt Pearl was blessed with an abundance of humor. When it came time for the invitation, all stood as the strains of 'Just as I Am' wafted through the sanctuary. In her haste to dress for the church service, Mama Davis had neglected to zip her skirt, but the top button kept it together—until she stood for the final hymn. The button went flying and the skirt dropped to the floor. Aunt Ora carefully guided Mama Davis back to a sitting position and proceeded to retrieve the skirt from the floor. But Aunt Pearl reacted differently. Overcome with laughter she sat back down, folded her arms, and placed them on the pew in front of her. Her head went down to her folded arms and she began to shake uncontrollably. Smothering her laughter, she stayed in this position for quite some time. The evangelist, thinking that Aunt Pearl was in the throes of having a life-changing experience, extended the invitation for several verses. And when she didn't move to the front, he extended it even more. Family members said that was the longest invitation in the history of the First

Baptist Church. Mama Davis went home chagrined; the evangelist went home sad because he had lost another soul to the devil; and Aunt Pearl went home still laughing.

Nice funeral coat

I have known Tom and Bonnie Hearon for a long time. I first knew them as collegiate ministers and then as missionaries. Somewhere in the mix I was the faculty advisor for Tom's doctoral project. Some of the most humorous things happen at the least humorous times such as at funerals. Tom sent me the following story about his father's funeral. "When my father died, my brother, Doug, and I selected some clothes to dress Dad in for his funeral. We left them hanging in the closet. On Wednesday morning the two of us went to the funeral home to make the arrangements. When we arrived, the funeral director asked us if we had brought the clothes. We had not thought of them that day, so Doug said that he would bring them back later. When we left there, we had other errands to run, to make arrangements with the cemetery, and to clear Dad's room at his nursing home. By the time we got home, I was worn out. Doug said that he would take the clothes back to the funeral home, so I pulled them out of the closet. Soon he was on his way. The days were filled with many family activities. Thursday night arrived quickly as we prepared for visitation at the funeral home. I was getting dressed when I realized that I had made a big mistake. I telephoned the funeral-home director. When I told him, he could not suppress a laugh. He said that he would check on the problem and would get back with me. The problem was that Dad was wearing my sports coat. I wanted it back if possible. I knew that the possibility was small, but I was at least going to try. When the director called me back, he told me that because the coat was much too large, they had to cut out the back. So the coat was ruined. As we stood over the coffin and looked at our father, it was hard for us to contain a smile, knowing our secret. In fact, the last words my brother said to our father before the funeral, as we looked over the casket together were, 'Nice coat.'"

Conclusion

A Serious Word

If you have had a laugh on me, then my mission in writing this book has been accomplished. Humorist Victor Borge once said, "If I have caused just one person to wipe away a tear of laughter, that's my reward." I agree.

A quote began appearing on the Internet around 2000 under the title, "Things I've Learned" and originally was attributed to Andy Rooney, veteran commentator for the television program, *60 Minutes*. Even though his staff denied that he ever said it, still it serves as a good summary for my conclusion. "I've learned . . . that no matter how serious your life requires you to be, everyone needs a friend to act goofy with."

Thanks for allowing me to be "goofy" with you. Looking back at funny times has been the best therapy I could have ever imagined. Some tend to be funnier as we look back than they ever were in actual experience. In his book, *Stories I Couldn't Tell When I was a Pastor,* Bruce McIver, wrote, "The beauty of hindsight is that it affords us the luxury of absorbing and appreciating what we missed the first time."[1]

I plan to continue looking for humor along my way to heaven. I recommend that you do so as well. The book's subtitle indicates I had planned to keep writing this book until the end of my life, or at least until I was a little closer to my arrival in heaven. However, the unexpected illnesses and deaths of some close colleagues and friends in recent days sobered me again to the uncertainty of tomorrow and the urgency of doing today what we deem important. So while the funny things that happen to me on my way to heaven have not ceased, I thought I would get them to a publisher and into print while it was yet day. If the Lord tarries and allows me many more days on this earth, perhaps there will be a sequel to this book. Or maybe I'll just keep posting my future funny stories on my web site:

www.discipleallnations.org.

Until then, keep on laughing. It beats the heck out of crying.

[1] Bruce McIver, *Stories I Couldn't Tell When I Was a Pastor* (Dallas: Word Publishing, 1991), 2

Appendix: Quotes without Footnotes[1]

"Humor is emotional chaos remembered in tranquility."
                                                    -James Thurber.

"A well-developed sense of humor is the pole that adds balance to your steps as you walk the tightrope of life."
                                                    -William A. Ward

"Humor is the identification of dignity."
                                                    -Charles Chaplin

"A sense of humor . . . is needed armor. Joy in one's heart and some laughter on one's lips is a sign that the person down deep has a pretty good grasp of life."
                                                    -Hugh Sidey

"Laughter is medicine to the weary bones."
                                                    -Carl Sandburg

"Through humor, you can soften some of the worst blows that life delivers. And once you find laughter, no matter how painful your situation might be, you can survive it."
                                                    -Bill Cosby

"A sense of humor is part of the art of leadership, of getting along with people, of getting things done."
                                                    -Dwight D. Eisenhower

"Laughter is the natural sound of childhood."
                                                    -Alvin Schwartz

"Humor is a rubber sword—it allows you to make a point without drawing blood."

-Mary Hirsch

"Wrinkles should merely indicate where the smiles have been."

-Mark Twain

"It is bad to suppress laughter. It goes back down and spreads to your hips."

-Fred Allen

"This is the best—to laugh with someone because you both think the same things are funny."

-Gloria Vanderbilt

"Nobody ever died of laughter."

-Max Beerbohm

"Humor and creativity are intimately related—there is a connection between HAHA and AHA."

-Joel Goodman

"Love may make the world go around, but laughter keeps us from getting dizzy."

-Donald Dochert

"Beware of those who laugh at nothing or everything."

-Arnold H. Glasgow

"When humor goes, there goes civilization."

-Erma Bombeck

"Does God have a sense of humor? He must have if He made us."

-Jackie Gleason

"You grow up the day you have your first real laugh—at yourself."

-Ethel Barrymore

"The freedom of any society varies proportionately with the volume of its laughter."

-Zero Mostel

"If a man insisted always on being serious, and never allowed himself a bit of fun and relaxation, he would go mad or become unstable without knowing it."

-Herodotus

"Laughter is like a muscle; if you don't use it, it begins to atrophy."

-Jay Leno

"A leader without a sense of humor is like the grass mower at the cemetery—he has a lot of people under him, but nobody is paying him any attention."

-Bob Ross

"At the height of laughter, the universe is flung into a kaleidoscope of new possibilities."

-Jean Houston

"Humor is not a trick, not jokes. Humor is a presence in the world—like grace—and shines on everybody."

-Garrison Keillor

139

"After God created the world, He created man and woman. And then to keep the whole thing from collapsing, he created humor."

-Ernie Hoberecht

"Laughter gives us distance. It allows us to step back from an event, deal with it and then move on."

-Bob Newhart

"Laughter is free, legal, has no calories, no cholesterol, no preservatives, no artificial ingredients, and is absolutely safe."

-Dale Irvin

"People will pay more to be entertained than educated."

-Johnny Carson

"Laughter is a tranquilizer with no side effects."

-Arnold Glasow

"If I can get you to laugh with me, you like me better, which makes you more open to my ideas."

-John Cleese

"Humor is the oil that keeps the engine of society from getting overheated."

-Mary McNorton

"Humor is a proof of faith."

-Charles Schulz

"A person without a sense of humor is like a wagon without springs. It's jolted by every pebble on the road."

-Henry Ward Beecher

"No matter what your heartache may be, laughing helps you forget it for a few seconds."

-Red Skelton

"No mind is thoroughly well organized that is deficient in a sense of humor."

-Samuel Coleridge

"Shared laughter creates a bond of friendship. When people laugh together, they cease to be young and old, teacher and pupils, worker and boss. They become a single group of human beings."

-W. Lee Grant

"It's hard to create humor because of the competition from the real world."

-Peter's Almanac.

"The person who can bring the spirit of laughter into a room is indeed blessed."

-Bennett Alfred Cerf

"Dogs laugh, but they laugh with their tails."

-Max Forrester Eastman

"The most thoroughly wasted of all days is that on which one has not laughed."

-Nicolas de Chamfort

"Not a shred of evidence exists in favor of the idea that life is serious."

-Brendan Gill

"Laughter is a holy thing. It is as sacred as music and silence and solemnity, maybe more sacred. Laughter is like a prayer, like a bridge over which creatures tiptoe to meet each other. Laughter is like mercy; it heals. When you can laugh at yourself, you are free."

-Ted Loder

[1]Quotes taken from the Internet and from *Laffirmations: 1,001 Ways to Add Humor to Your Life and Work,* Joel Goodman, Deerfield Beach, Florida: Health Communications, Inc. 1995.

Order more copies of

Mud Hen in a Peacock Parade

Call toll free: 1-800-747-0738

Visit: *www.hannibalbooks.com*

Email: *orders@hannibalbooks.com*

FAX: 1-888-252-3022

Mail copy of form below to:

Hannibal Books

P.O. Box 461592

Garland, TX 75046

Number of copies desired _____

Multiply number of copies by $14.95

Subtotal _____

Please add $4.00 for postage and handling for first book and add $1.00 for each additional book in the order.

Shipping and handling$_____

Texas residents add 8.25% sales tax $_____

Total order $_____

Mark method of payment:

check enclosed _____

Credit card# _____

exp. date_____ (Visa, MasterCard, Discover, American Express accepted)

Name _____

Address _____

City State, Zip _____

Phone _____ FAX _____

Email _____